For James,
my hero and my love,
who helps me rejoice in each day.

What's After Assessment?

Follow-Up Instruction for Phonics, Fluency, and Comprehension

Kathleen Strickland

HEINEMANN
Portsmouth, NH

Heinemann
A division of Reed Elsevier Inc.
361 Hanover Street
Portsmouth, NH 03801–3912
www.heinemann.com

Offices and agents throughout the world

© 2005 by Kathleen Strickland

The author and publisher wish to thank those who have generously given permission to reprint borrowed material:

Figure 2–4: "Ideas for Various Partner Strategy Explorations" from *Comprehension: Strategic Instruction for K–3 Students* by Gretchen Owocki. Copyright © 2003 by Gretchen Owocki. Published by Heinemann, a division of Reed Elsevier, Inc., Portsmouth, NH. All rights reserved.

Credits for borrowed material continue on p. x.

Library of Congress Cataloging-in-Publication Data
Strickland, Kathleen.
    What's after assessment? : follow-up instruction for phonics, fluency, and comprehension / Kathleen Strickland.
       p. cm.
    Includes bibliographical references and index.
    ISBN 0-325-00572-9 (alk. paper)
    1. Reading (Elementary). 2. Reading comprehension. 3. Reading—Aids and devices. I. Title.

LB1573.S894 2005
372.41—dc22
                                                    2004030645

Editor: James Strickland
Production: Vicki Kasabian
Cover design: Catherine Hawkes, Cat & Mouse Design
Typesetter: Tom Allen, Pear Graphic Design
Manufacturing: Steve Bernier

Printed in the United States of America on acid-free paper
09 08 07 06   VP   5

Contents

Appendixes

Preface

I've always believed in the power of writing to represent thought and bring clarity to ideas. During the writing of this book, I've also learned that the very act of writing can be a lifeline to cling to as we try to make sense of life's difficult periods. The two years I spent writing this book were personally challenging ones, to say the least, but I was blessed to have people in my life who supported my progress and were patient and encouraging as the book came together.

The person most responsible for helping me finish is my husband, and editor, Jim Strickland. Jim's always been my writing teacher, doing what good teachers of writing do, convincing me that I can, responding to my writing as an interested reader, and encouraging me to keep writing. He's a talented editor, and I thank him for helping make this book a reality.

I'd like to thank all the teachers who have shared their ideas, practices, time, and expertise with me over the years. I've also learned a great deal from the graduate students in the Reading program at Slippery Rock University, talented and dedicated teachers, like Joe Rubaker and Linda Scott. Their questions and thoughts are represented throughout this book in a variety of ways. I'd also like to thank Janet Hoffman and Nancy Castor, wonderful principals at Hempfield Elementary School in Greenville, Pennsylvania; the actual idea behind this book grew out of my years working with teachers in their school. Janet and Nancy encourage teaching to students' needs and provide time and support for discussing appropriate instructional possibilities that will help students progress as readers.

I especially want to thank Amy Walker for years of friendship and for long hours discussing best practices for teaching reading in general and the "If . . . Then" section of this book in particular. I'd also like to thank those who helped me take photos for the book: the teachers at Connequenessing Valley Elementary School, the SRU Child Care Center, and Laura Steiger, a practicing Title I teacher who keeps me grounded.

I'd like to thank my friends at Heinemann who have become such an important part of our lives—Maura Sullivan for her brilliant guidance, Vicki Kasabian for her production skills, Leigh Peake for her steadfast support, Lois Bridges for her intuitive wisdom, Melissa Inglis for her proofreading expertise, and Eric Chalek for his constant enthusiasm. You are all very special.

CHAPTER ONE

Planning for Instruction

I hear teachers saying, "I've done the assessments and found what this reader can do and that she is having difficulty with fluency (or drawing conclusions, or making inferences, or seeing a purpose for reading in his/her life). I'm aware of some instructional strategies for teaching reading skills, but after exhausting them, or discovering that they aren't making the necessary difference, I feel lost. So, what do I do now? What's next?"

This is a reasonable question, and one that informed teachers ask frequently. The strategies in this book are not magical formulas, but they may help teachers decide what to do next. The strategies are presented so that teachers can see them for what they are and appreciate their place in the development of reading strategies—the meaningful construction of concepts and connections, the discovery of the story, if you will. As we've learned from Vygotsky (1978), learners must be in a state of readiness, recognizing the purpose of any activity, and without that readiness, strategies turn into yet one more batch of school day exercises.

After assessing readers' needs, teachers want a resource that clearly and logically provides teaching ideas, activities, and appropriate instructional guidelines for developing readers. This book provides concrete classroom strategies that help teachers decide what to do next. Too often curricular programs and textbook publishers think that instruction comes first. But knowing each of our students as individual readers, and planning lessons based on their needs, is far more important. To give us a window into the mind of each reader, we assess at the start of the school year and at regular intervals throughout the year, using assessment tools such as surveys, anecdotal records, checklists, miscue analysis, and running records (see Goodman and Burke [1972], Strickland and Strickland [2000], Wilde [2000], and Clay [2000]). As we begin to form pictures of each reader based on these assessments, we identify individual strengths and needs so that we can tailor our instruction to facilitate each reader's growth.

How to Use This Book

This book helps teachers distinguish between activities and strategies. Activities are ideas that help readers develop appropriate strategies for reading. Sometimes the reader is aware that a particular activity is supporting the learning of a strategy (for instance, using a bookmark under a line of text to help with fluent reading, tracking). Other times, the reader is not aware of all the purposes of an activity, but strategies are learned through the activity (for instance, fluency is aided by the repeated reading of readers' theatre, but the reader is aware of the primary purpose, which is the enjoyment of the text and the performance of the text for an audience). By cross-referencing and indexing, teachers can access teaching strategies, activities, and appropriate instructional guidelines for developing readers. Some suggestions will be appropriate for whole-class activities; others will address the individual needs of the reader.

Becoming Strategic Readers

Children do learn to read by reading, but what teachers need to do is support them as they read, so they can do what real readers do. This isn't done through skills and drills, phonics worksheets, or sequencing activities. It's done through books and talk and listening and thinking. Along the way teachers can use techniques like mapping, retelling, and graphic organizers, not as exercises, but as ways to help readers think about the text. Unfortunately, kids often see this as busy work, as something teachers make them do for a grade. Teachers need to help children see the purpose in these techniques and find ways to assist them in becoming strategic readers. If kids see a purpose and find that mapping is helpful, it empowers them—it helps them do what other readers do. Kids and teachers alike have to accept the fact that not all techniques work equally well for all readers, even if those readers have similar needs. Students need opportunities to make decisions about what works and what doesn't. They need to take control of their learning, take risks, know it is okay to back up and try something else—all this while they're enjoying reading. It's like a well-orchestrated ballet; the teacher may be the choreographer, but the readers bring life to the dance, or meaning to the text.

Individualized Instruction

Sometimes we have the luxury of planning one-on-one instruction, but often in a class of twenty-five students, we find that our instruction must be delivered in small groups or even as whole-class instruction. Even instruction in groups can be individualized if we work to teach readers strategies rather than fill our instructional time with a string of activities. Often I talk with teachers who ask, "What's next?" After assessing, and using some common activities for instruction, they're often at a loss as to how to provide the appropriate support for each student. Only by assisting what students do as they read, by looking through the window of miscue analysis, can teachers know how students are approaching the act of reading. Only by talking with students, usually informally as one reader to another, can a teacher understand how students view themselves as readers and what place they see literacy has in their lives. Only then, after the information gathering has taken place, will teachers be ready to make decisions about appropriate instructional strategies.

The ideas in this book are a compilation of teaching ideas to help teachers make instructional decisions based on what they know about their students. It is not a program—*teachers* remain the professional decision makers with this book. However, it is a resource book for teachers. These ideas for teaching are based on a belief that reading is a meaning-making activity and that proficient readers make meaning by using three cueing systems— *semantic cues* (meaning cues or context), *syntactic cues* (grammatical cues coming from knowledge of the language), and *graphic cues* (letter–sound correspondences and word patterns) (Weaver 2002). Each of these cueing systems is essential, and as we teach children to be strategic readers, we must find ways to help them use all three simultaneously, not overutilizing any one to the exclusion of the other two. As we teach reading, we must, through our example, help children understand that all reading is making meaning, so our lessons must therefore be meaningful and not just based on skills in isolation. We learn to read by reading, Frank Smith (1994) tells us, so all reading instruction must be conducted within the process of authentic reading situations. Practice is important, so to grow as readers, children must read. These lessons are part of reading instruction that includes time for independent reading of the child's choice, shared reading, guided reading, and reading aloud to children.

Setting Up Environment for Success

Before deciding how to support developing readers, certain assumptions about reading and learning to read must be made. Some of these assumptions are outlined in ideas adapted from Cora Lee Five and Marie Dionisio (1999):

Beliefs About Learners

1. We view struggling readers as capable and accept what they can do and are interested in.
2. We focus on struggling readers' strengths, not weaknesses.
3. We know and value struggling readers' individual leaning styles.
4. We accept that all children will learn but at different times and in different ways.

Beliefs About the Reading Process

1. We reinforce the concept that reading is constructing meaning.
2. We view mistakes as signs of learning in progress rather than indicators of failure.
3. We view reading as purposeful and interesting.

Beliefs About Our Instruction

1. We help struggling readers choose books they're interested in and can read.
2. We base assessment on individual growth and achievement rather than on standardized test scores.
3. We base instruction on individual needs and development.
4. We help students set long- and short-term goals and help students self-assess.
5. We give struggling learners time to try new strategies while they are engaged in meaningful reading and time to think and talk about how those strategies worked.
6. We create instructional groups that are flexible and temporary, based on needs and/or interests of the learners.
7. We accept that not all strategies are equally effective for all readers.

Retrospective Miscue Analysis

Retrospective Miscue Analysis (RMA) helps readers see themselves as readers and in the process "revalue" themselves as readers (K. Goodman 1991). RMA demonstrates to readers that reading is making meaning from text. Many struggling readers [mistakenly] think reading is mainly decoding words and pronouncing syllables, [rather than] . . . making sense of a text by using a variety of appropriate strategies (Moore and Gilles 2005, 1). In RMA, readers with their teacher at their side examine their reading through the "windows" of their miscues and in the process begin to understand and evaluate how they read. "For students and teachers alike, the analysis process is informative and enjoyable because there is no competition for a correct answer; what the reader has to say is validated by the RMA partner or partners" (1). As with miscue analysis, the reader is audiotaped during RMA sessions and asked to retell the text. As Rita Moore and Carol Gilles explain, "The process of RMA is a two-part sequence: an initial reading and retelling session is followed by a conversation about the reading and the retelling. During the initial session, a student reads aloud from a challenging text [one chosen slightly above instructional level] while the teacher listens to and marks the *miscues*—the unexpected responses to text in the oral reading. . . . Some examples of miscues are substitutions, insertions, and omissions" (2). However, RMA uses a follow-up session in which the reader listens to the taped reading along with his or her teacher, who notes the student's patterns of reading behavior to share at the RMA session. A few days later at the RMA session the reader is encouraged, first, to examine his miscues to determine whether or not they changed the meaning of the text, and second, to decide what strategies might be most effective in helping him monitor for meaning. Together the reader and the teacher discuss each miscue. Did it make sense? Did the miscue change the meaning of the text? Was it corrected? Did it need to be corrected? And, what was the reader thinking at the time the miscue was read? Using this technique over time helps readers develop strategies that are appropriate through reading. The reading process becomes less of a mystery and students feel more in control and, maybe more important, students begin to revalue themselves as readers.

Prisca Martens (1998) tells the story of Michael who used only two strategies when reading—sounding out and asking the teacher. His goal was to read words better though he did not see himself as a good reader. In his first RMA session, he and Martens looked at the miscues he made while reading *The Three Little Pigs*. Michael used "wolf called" and "wolf cried" interchangeably and saw these miscues as wrong. In their first few sessions together, Martens talked with him about these miscues being "smart" miscues because they made sense, and she proceeded to use strategy lessons suggested by Goodman, Watson, and Burke (1996).

A month later, when Michael heard himself reading another story, he accepted his miscue of reading, "said Owl," instead of the text version, "he said," as one that a proficient reader would make. He began to discuss the decisions authors make when creating meaning and how readers sometime make those decisions themselves. As their RMA sessions continued over the following months, Martens and Michael discussed what they were seeing in Michael's reading and the strategies of proficient readers. Michael began to consciously monitor himself for meaning and began to be more confident and view himself as a good reader.

Starting at the Beginning by Identifying Strengths and Needs

Our responsibility as teachers for reading instruction begins the first day our students walk into our classrooms. Along with that instruction begins assessment so we can be aware of what our students know and what is appropriate for us to teach. As we gather data we begin to see the pieces of a puzzle come together, each bit of information providing another piece of the big picture. In books, such as my own *Making Assessment Elementary* (Strickland and Strickland 2000), as well as *Running Records for Classroom Teachers* (Clay 2000), *Miscue Analysis Made Easy* (Wilde 2000), and *Classroom Based Assessment* (Hill, Rubtic, and Norwick 1998), we learn how to gather data through instruments such as reading surveys given to children and parents, the use of checklists and anecdotal records, and most important, the administration and analysis of running records and miscue analysis. What comes next is deciding how to organize this data so it tells us something about our readers and then making instructional decisions based on what we discover.

One of the first steps in this analysis is constructing what is commonly called a *strength and needs list*, which is used to develop goals for instruction. For instance, based on assessment from running records, I might be able to determine that Jordan, who is nine years old and in third grade, has a first-grade instructional reading level, and reads simple books at a primer level independently. I know such determinations are quite arbitrary depending on interest and ease during the assessment sessions, and this gives me only a place to start, not information about what strategies Jordan uses or what I need to help him with. Through the use of running records as well as other tools I know the following:

Student's Name: **Jordan**

Grade: **3**

Testing and Observation

Use of second grade developmental reading assessment (DRA): Level 4 (92 percent accuracy)

Use of usual assessments such as running record, surveys, checklists, anecdotal records, artifacts

Additional assessment information, including

- An IEP for speech (expressive and receptive language test average; articulation problems)
- Hearing screening (shows a problem)
- Reading Recovery in first grade (made significant gains one-on-one)
- Retained in kindergarten
- Problem with absenteeism (has moved several times)

Strengths

- Writes what he hears and speaks; has made connection with oral language and letter–sound relationships
- Writes about what is important in his life
- Is able to read higher-level material silently
- Uses a variety of strategies to attack a word, especially beginning sounds

Needs

- Overuses sound/symbol in writing
- Has limited knowledge of sight words
- Has halting choppy oral reading (see speech assessment)
- Does not see himself as a reader/writer
- Does not make use of strengths

Goals

1. Develop more effective word analysis skill, with less emphasis on sound/symbol and more emphasis on context
2. Increase sight vocabulary (reading and writing)
3. Improve silent fluency rate
4. Improve confidence as a reader and as a writer
5. Increase time spent reading

So, now I have a place to start. I've begun my assessment of Jordan as a reader and I know what he can do and what he needs help with. Based on this information, I can begin planning my instruction so it will meet Jordan's needs. I know Jordan is only one student in my classroom of twenty-five and they all have needs, but this information will help with focused minilessons, flexible grouping, and instruction during guided reading and one-to-one instruction throughout the week. It will also help me to plan activities and facilitate experiences that will help Jordan and others. In other words, my instruction is focused on children's particular needs, rather than a one-size-fits-all program that cannot make instructional decisions that fit a child's growth and development as a reader.

Now based on Jordan's needs I can begin to plan for his instruction. That is when I can use the ideas in this book in ways that are tailored for this particular student and create instructional possibilities.

Instructional Possibilities

1. Build confidence/interest as a reader and writer
   - Read high-interest material with a reading partner; emphasize silent reading and discussion—this will lessen attention to his speech problem (Chapter 2)
   - Use technology for reading and writing—use computers to support a child's writing (Chapter 5)
   - Use shared reading—listening comprehension—high-interest stories at his age level (chapter books); have him follow along and track as he is listening (Chapter 7)
2. Increase time spent reading
   - Combine reading and writing as much as possible; use language experience approach during writing workshop (Chapter 7). Have Jordan read back what he has dictated; work on story elements with his own stories
   - Build on personal interests (Chapter 5)
3. Develop more effective use of multiple strategies
   - Emphasize meaning over all other strategies; try cloze activities, first with familiar text and then with unfamiliar text. Let Jordan try this silently first (Chapter 8)
   - Encourage him to skip words when reading silently and then go back; model this for him. Give him the initial consonant if necessary (Chapter 2)

- Emphasize the way words look rather than the way they sound (patterns, words in words, length) (Chapters 3 and 4)
4. Improve silent fluency rate
   - Have Jordan read his own writing repeatedly when revising and publishing on the computer (Chapter 5)
   - During SSR have Jordan read silently for five minutes and then discuss with an adult. Give him time to get involved in the story without interruption, but stop to reinforce meaning (Chapter 2)
   - Avoid attention to oral fluency (Chapter 5)
5. Increase sight vocabulary
   - Use spelling dictionary to record high-frequency words he needs (alphabet journal) (Chapters 3 and 4)
   - Use high-frequency words as spelling words (self-chosen) (Chapter 4)

Another example of an analysis of a child's strengths and needs can be seen by looking at second grader Christine:

Student's Name: **Christine**

Grade: **2**

Assessments included running records, surveys, checklists, anecdotal records, speech teacher's report.

Strengths

- Generates copious text when writing
- Has a cooperative and hardworking attitude
- Connects story to life
- Writes words as they sound
- Chooses books
- Has good listening comprehension

Needs

- Has little ability to retell—focuses on details rather than theme or gist of the story
- Does not read for meaning—substitutes words that do not make sense
- Uses few strategies when reading—tries only to sound out (letters and sounds)
- Is easily frustrated

Goals

1. Develop a more positive attitude toward reading and help her see herself as a reader and a writer
2. See reading as meaning making
3. Develop retelling skills
4. Develop word analysis skills other than phonics, especially use of context

5. Encourage active comprehension (making predictions, risking a guess)

Instructional Possibilities

1. See herself as a reader
   - Use high-interest websites such as author sites (Jan Brett, Marc Brown, etc.)
   - Use computer programs such as Kid Pix and Hyper Studio to produce her own text
   - Keep track of favorite books using a reading log (those read to her as well as those read independently); provide opportunities to share favorites with others (book club)
2. Reading as meaning-making
   - Focus on silent reading first, then discussion, then rereading orally, then retelling
   - Begin by using high-interest books chosen by her and read with an adult
3. Retelling
   - Have her retell books read aloud to her
   - Discuss characters and story plot first; use puppets, props with others
   - Progress to simple story mapping
4. Develop word analysis skills
   - Cloze activities—begin with selections from books shared that are high interest selections, some blanks have beginning sounds. Discuss strategies (how did you know that word?)
   - Attend to the way words look—word play—patterns, word families, and so on (using stories and books she is engaged in)
5. Encourage active comprehension
   - Share reading and discussion
   - Read her own writing—take Christine's stories, discuss elements, edit with an adult, publish using computer programs and read (display and share if possible)
   - Participate in literature circle using a novel that is appropriate for interest and age (will need help reading, but should encourage independent response)

Matching Assessed Needs with Instruction— "If a child . . . , Then . . ."

Often teachers appreciate ideas or reminders of possible approaches that can be taken during reading instruction to meet the needs of developing readers. The chart that follows identifies some common findings about readers' approaches to text and the act of reading. Some instructional possibilities follow each description of an assessment finding, all of which are found in this book, listed by name in the Index and Contents.

The chart by no means encompasses every behavior exhibited by readers, and teachers are encouraged to add their own ideas under each category, but it does provide ideas and begins to sort out possibilities for appropriate instruction based on assessed needs.

If . . . Then Chart

If a child (based on assessment(s)) . . . , **then** (some instructional possibilities are) . . .

If a child reads word by word, then

Present opportunities for rereading
- Repeated reading
- Readers' theatre
- Environmental print/reading and writing about their world

Work on prereading so student makes predictions and reads to confirm or adjust predictions
- Pretelling
- Anticipation guides
- Webbing
- Activate prior knowledge
- Set purpose for reading

Model fluent reading
- Shared reading
- Paired reading (reading buddies)
- Read-alouds
- Tracking
- Adjusting reading rate

If a child reads words letter by letter, then

Model fluent reading
- Shared reading
- News and announcements

Help child see words as wholes
- Word sorts
- Word walls
- Alphabet books (check letter recognition)
- Personal dictionary
- Word of the day
- List–group–share (LGS)
- Visual–auditory–kinesthetic–tactile (VAKT) approach
- Tracking
- Cloze

Help child see word patterns
- Onset/rime
- Structural analysis

If a child reads slowly, but comprehends, then

Present authentic reasons for rereading
- Readers' theatre
- Writing text for struggling readers
- Rereading

Model fluent reading
- Shared reading
- Read-alouds
- Adjusting reading rate

Present opportunities for student to read fluently with support
- Choral reading
- Computer reading
- Paired reading with fluent readers
- Tape-recorded reading
- Games such as Leap Pad
- Tracking

If a child reads so slowly that comprehension is compromised, then

Take time for prereading
- Activate prior knowledge
- Set purpose for reading
- Anticipation guides
- Guided instruction
- KWL
- Create a scenario

Model fluent reading and attend to meaning before having student read independently
- Think-alouds

Make sure text is at appropriate level
- Choosing book at independent/instructional level

If a child reads fluently but can't retell, then

Make sure student understands how to retell
- Retelling
- Webbing/mapping
- Interpretive questions
- Story frames

- Semantic webbing

Make sure student is constructing meaning while reading
- Imagery
- Predicting
- Guided reading
- Reciprocal teaching
- Directed reading-thinking activity (DRTA)
- Adjusting reading rates

If a child reads fluently but misses many details, then

Help reader see that he should examine text and reread when necessary
- Mapping
- Webbing
- Reciprocal teaching
- Context clues, rereading, and skipping
- Self-questioning (if reader can't identify main idea or purpose)

Discuss story/text with others and revisit texts during discussion
- Literature circles
- Pair–think–share
- Linguistic roulette
- Artful artist
- Write and Share[2]

If a child reads fluently but can't (or sometimes doesn't) identify main idea or purpose, then

Help reader bring meaning to text, connect to experience and previous knowledge, and organize the elements of the text during and after reading
- Story mapping
- Literature circles
- Compare and contrast charts
- Write and Share[2]
- Artful artist
- Paraphrasing
- Asking for help
- Venn diagram
- Response logs
- Summarizing/retelling
- Connecting

If a child isn't able to make inferences (recalls literally), then

Help reader realize that when making meaning she must put pieces of information together to make sense of text; help reader see not everything is stated directly
- Think-alouds
- Comprehension strategy framework
- Literature circles
- Inferential strategy
- Write and Share[2]
- Response logs
- Say something
- Summarizing/retelling
- Connecting

If a child can decode but uses only letter sounds, then

Help reader see that decoding words involves multiple strategies such as onsets/rimes, words within words, structural analysis, context clues
- Word sorts
- Onset/rime
- Cloze
- Word bank
- Making words
- Contextual analysis
- Finding little words in big words
- Writing

If a child guesses at words using only initial consonant sound as cues, then

Help reader see words as wholes and in the context of an authentic reading situation
- Cloze activities during shared reading
- Computer reading programs
- Language experience

Help reader use multiple strategies for decoding
- Word families
- Word sorts
- Cloze
- Word banks
- Making words
- Contextual analysis
- Bag words
- Writing

If a child has problems with sight words, then

Help reader build a repertoire of sight words by connecting words to life/experience for long-term memory
- Word walls
- Personal dictionary
- Bag words

Demonstrate to reader that sight words are usually built from reading, not before reading
- Word study after reading
- Writing

If a child has problems choosing appropriate books, then

Teach strategies for choosing books based on interest and ability
- Choosing books
- Reading buddies
- Sharing books
- Owning books

If a child has little interest in reading, then

Help reader to discuss purposes for reading in his/her life
- Environmental print
- Literacy play boxes
- Books about me
- Interactive reading (reading with students)
- Computer stories or reading games
- Word games (word bingo, stick person, Scrabble)
- Reading aloud to child
- Shared reading
- Owning books
- Jackdaws

If a child has little confidence in reading ability, then

Help child see him/herself as a reader
- Read to younger children
- Reading logs (list of books read)
- Choosing appropriate books
- Language experience (reading books written by child)
- Choral reading
- Shared reading

Emphasize reading strengths
- Use strengths/needs list to begin with what students can do

- Share strengths/needs list with parents and child
- Work on goals together

If a child pays little attention to print in the world, then

Help child see purpose of print
- Environmental print
- Work with names
- Reading the room (a form of environmental print)
- Literacy play boxes
- Word games
- Language experience

If a child guesses at unknown words, using no graphic cues, then

Help reader pay attention to the visual aspects of word identification while still using syntactic and semantic cues
- Cloze with initial consonant sound
- Finding little words in big words
- Structural analysis
- Onset/rime
- Word sorts
- Writing

If a child doesn't attend to story or attention wanders during reading, then

Help reader see reading as a meaningful activity
- Interest inventory
- Reading own writing
- Choosing appropriate books
- DRTA
- Reading buddies
- SSR with buddy (pair–think–share)
- Language experience

If a child reads words he knows but stops at every new or unfamiliar word, then

Help child realize reading is not just reading words, help learn to use all three cueing systems
- Cloze activities
- Use of prediction before and after reading
- Guided reading
- Think-alouds

If a child memorizes text during repeated readings, then

Help child pay attention to words in text
- Working with words using a familiar story, personal dictionary, and so on
- Scrambled sentences
- Tracking with finger
- Computer versions of story with highlighted text
- Computer games such as Leap Pad that use pencil for tracking

If a child has difficulty tracking, loses place, then

Help child practice reading fluently using aids that train the eyes to process left to right, line by line
- Computer versions of story with highlighted text
- Leap Pad reading games
- Tracking with finger
- Shared reading
- Tracking with a bookmark

If a child doesn't recognize new words built on known words, then

Help reader learn that words are not always individual letters, but often have parts
- Structural analysis
- Word sorts
- Making words
- Word games
- Rhyming words
- Word families
- News and announcements chart

If a child has difficulty with letter–sound correspondence, then

Help reader learn high-frequency letter–sound correspondence (consonants) in the context of real reading situations or as a result of examining text in real reading situations
- Letters in the context of real reading
- Tongue twisters
- Nursery rhymes

If a child reads quickly but inaccurately and with limited comprehension, then

Help child read at a pace that supports comprehension; help child read for meaning
- DRTA

- Comprehension strategy framework
- Anticipation guide
- Guided reading
- Pair–think–share
- Reciprocal teaching

If a child reads only one genre, or one type of book, then

Help child to broaden interests and experiences with books, while respecting choice and interest
- Read aloud from various genres
- Share books
- Introduce books through book talks
- Recommend or suggest a book similar but one step removed (i.e., from *Goosebumps* to another type of mystery)

If a child has difficulty reading for information, then

Help child develop techniques for reading nonfiction, which is different from reading text with a story grammar
- Think-alouds
- Reciprocal teaching
- Anticipation guides
- KWL
- Webbing
- Jackdaws

If a child has little knowledge of the alphabet, then

Make learning alphabet interesting and fun (letters need not be learned in order)
- Songs, nursery rhymes, and choral reading
- Alphabet books
- Letters in names
- Alphabet blocks
- Alphabet sound word examples
- Magnetic letters and other Everyday Phonics
- Writing letters in shaving cream
- Handheld games and other Everyday Phonics
- Letter detective
- Letters in writing

If a child has little knowledge of books, then

Help reader feel comfortable with text and book handling
- Read aloud with child (shared reading modeled after bedtime reading)

- Older reading buddies
- Owning books
- Library card

If a child does not recognize word units, then

Help reader realize that print is made up of words that match speech
- Shared reading
- News and announcements chart
- Word wall
- Writing

If a child has difficulty matching letters with corresponding sounds, then

Help reader realize that words are made up of letters that correspond with speech sounds
- Counting words in speech
- Clapping syllables
- Sound boxes
- Alphabet sound word examples
- Word games—match word with beginning letter
- Rhyming
- Rhyming books
- Everyday phonics (I-spy, alphabet cans, magnetic letters, etc.)

If a child needs or wishes to develop vocabulary, then

Help student devise methods of adding new words she encounters in context of reading to her reading/writing vocabulary
- Word maps
- Contextual analysis
- Word games
- Context-structure-sound-reference (CSSR)

CHAPTER TWO

Building Confidence

Changing Attitudes Toward Reading

My daughter, Laura, a special education and reading teacher, worked for several years as a tutor. She would work individually with struggling readers for an hour a week. Though challenging and often frustrating, Laura knew one hour of "instruction" wasn't very much. What she discovered, however, was that over time, one hour could make a difference if it was spent on real reading and helping a developing reader understand what reading actually is.

Courtney, a second grader, was nervous and unhappy about going for tutoring, already convinced she couldn't read. Her instruction in reading thus far, both at home and in school, was quite heavily phonics based, and when Courtney read, it was halting, word-by-word reading, with a heavy concentration on sounding out each individual word. What was interesting, however, was that even after a painfully long time getting through a sentence and what seemed forever to get the end of a passage, Courtney seemed to comprehend the story. She could retell and, although she missed many details, was able to tell the gist of the passage.

Laura identified her first and most important task in early sessions—this had to be an enjoyable hour or neither of them would get anywhere. Laura began by spending much of the time reading to Courtney, at first books Laura chose and the books Courtney requested. Then they did what any two real readers would do; they talked about the story—no teacher questions and answers—but what your friend and you do when you both read the same book or see the same movie. They discussed favorite parts, characters, actions, and connections to their lives. Not many sessions later, Courtney and Laura decided to refer to their time together as a book club rather than tutoring. Courtney felt more comfortable telling her friends she was going to book club after school, and she arrived at Laura's door with a smile.

Laura always spent some time reading to Courtney, but soon Courtney was volunteering to read a paragraph or page, haltingly at first, and gradually the interest in the story led her to use other strategies. Laura shared some suggestions with her, encouraged her to skip words, read ahead, to use what she knew about the story to help her predict what might make sense. She could even use her knowledge of phonics, especially beginning sounds, along with her understanding of the story and predictions to work at difficult words. But words were no longer the central focus, the story was.

Over the two years Laura and Courtney worked together, Courtney's parents were thrilled. They saw their daughter blossom into a confident, efficient reader. What's more, Courtney now enjoyed reading. She didn't gobble up books on her own, but she did read during her twenty-minute reading time most evenings and her reading performance at school really progressed. Her grades went up, which seemed to "prove" to Courtney that she could read.

Courtney learned to read by reading. It took time, patience, risk taking on both Courtney's and her teacher's part, but the fact is she began to see a purpose for reading, not to decode words, but to enjoy the story. Reading was "stories," not words, as Gary, another struggling reader, once discovered (Strickland 1995). When Courtney gradually learned that, she was then ready for Laura to teach her how to read more strategically, more efficiently. Courtney then had a reason for trying those strategies and did so in an atmosphere of support. Laura opened the door for Courtney, but stories walked her through it and she soon became another member of the "literacy club" (F. Smith 1988).

As children develop reading strategies they must have a positive attitude toward the process and see a place for reading in their lives. In this chapter, I share ideas that should help teachers support students as they learn to see themselves as readers.

Interest and Choice

It's important to find out first what children are interested in, what they like to read about, and actually provide opportunity for choice. Figures 2–1 (A–C) and 2–2 are examples of literacy surveys we could administer, but they'll only be of value if we use them to help us decide where to begin.

Choosing Books

As proficient readers, we know that we prefer to choose the books we will read, and we have strategies for making these choices—having a favorite author or genre, looking at the cover, reading reviews, reading the back cover, even considering print size or text length. We also choose books based on interest, mood, or need. Developing readers have a much more difficult time deciding which books to read, although we know that they

Your Thoughts About School

Name _____ Date _____

Age _____ Grade _____

1. In the morning, when you wake up, how do you feel about going to school? Why? _____
_____
_____

2. What are your favorite activities in school? _____
_____
_____

3. What do you like to learn about? _____
_____
_____

4. What do you think is easy to learn in school? Why is it easy? _____
_____
_____

5. What is hard to learn about or difficult to do in school? Why is it hard? _____
_____
_____

6. What have you done in school that you like to remember? _____
_____
_____

7. What have you done in school that you are most proud of? _____
_____
_____

8. What are your goals for this year? _____
_____
_____

9. What topics would you like to learn about this year? _____
_____
_____

10. What do you hope your teacher does this year? _____
_____
_____

Figure 2–1A Three student surveys inquiring about school, reading, and writing

What I Think About Reading

Name _____ Date _____

Age _____ Grade _____

1. When did you learn to read? Who taught you to read? _____
_____

2. How often do you read? _____
_____

3. What do you enjoy reading in school or at home? _____
_____

4. Do you have books of your own? If so, what are the titles of some of them? _____
_____

5. Who is your favorite author? Your favorite book? _____
_____

6. Do you like people to read aloud to you? (Your teacher, parent, older sister or brother, babysitter?)
_____

7. Do you like to read aloud or silently? Why? _____
_____

8. Do you go to the library? Do you have a library card? _____
_____

9. What do you think a good reader is? What do good readers do? _____
_____

10. Do you think you are a good reader? Why or why not? _____
_____

11. Do you think it's important to read? Why or why not? _____
_____

12. What do you want to learn about reading? _____
_____

Figure 2–1B

What I Think About Writing

Name _____ Date _____

Age _____ Grade _____

1. When did you learn to write? Who taught you to write? _____
_____
_____

2. What do you like to write about at home? _____
_____
_____

3. What do you like to write about at school? _____
_____
_____

4. What makes a person a good writer? What do good writers do? _____
_____
_____

5. Who do you think is a good writer? Why is he or she good? _____
_____
_____

6. What are some topics you like to write about? _____
_____
_____

7. Do you like to share your writing with other people? Why or why not? _____
_____
_____

8. Do you like to read the writing of other people in your class? Why or why not? _____
_____
_____

9. What do you think about your writing? _____
_____
_____

10. Do you think writing is important? Why or why not? _____
_____
_____

Figure 2–1C

> *Directions:* Read each of the following prompts aloud to each child (or children) and ask the child to circle or color the appropriate response.
>
> This is how I feel when:
>
> 1. Someone reads stories to me. ☺ ☻ ☹
> 2. I get a book for a present. ☺ ☻ ☹
> 3. I look at books by myself. ☺ ☻ ☹
> 4. I go to the library or bookstore. ☺ ☻ ☹
> 5. I read with someone in my family. ☺ ☻ ☹
> 6. I talk about books I've read. ☺ ☻ ☹
> 7. I look at the pictures in books or magazines. ☺ ☻ ☹
> 8. Someone tells me a story. ☺ ☻ ☹
> 9. I tell my favorite story to someone. ☺ ☻ ☹
> 10. I read a book with my friends in class. ☺ ☻ ☹

Figure 2–2 Primary reading attitude survey

have a much better chance of being successful as readers if they are reading books that interest them and ones they can read with a minimum of difficulty. Have you ever watched a young reader choose a book at a library or bookstore? They sometimes seem overwhelmed and just wander around aimlessly until they give up and randomly grab a book.

This type of behavior reminds me of a story about my son Jason when he was about eight years old. Our family, vacationing in Lake George, New York, was in a souvenir shop that ironed decals onto T-shirts. Our daughter, Laura, then six years old, took less than a minute to choose decal #36, three white kittens playing with a ball of yarn. Jason, on the other hand, hated making mistakes and found choices difficult. With over one hundred decals to choose from, I began to think we'd be there all day. Choice was so stressful for Jason that, after about twenty minutes and much pressure and prodding from the other members of the family, he was close to tears and I was feeling like an unfit mother. We left with no shirt for Jason and went to lunch so everyone could calm down. As the family was finishing their meals, I returned to the store, and considering Jason's age and interests, chose four decals I knew would be appropriate and ones to his liking. I wrote down numbers *8, 13, 21,* and *34* and gave them to Jason. He returned to the store and from these four choices, chose a basketball decal. As a mother and as a teacher, this experience taught me a valuable lesson about choice.

Choice is important, but we need to help children learn *how* to choose. Simple, but important lessons about choice include:

1. **Know your students.** Some children know what they like and are secure enough to take risks and experiment, like Laura. Others, like Jason, are born perfectionists and have difficulty with choice because

they're afraid they'll make the wrong one. Choice can be limited—whether choosing a book for a literature circle or for SSR, teachers can limit choice based on a number of criteria, such as

    a. Books available

    b. Reading level

    c. Topic

    d. Genre

A choice of one book from three possibilities still empowers the reader, and for some children, like Jason, limits the risks.

2. **Teach children how to make a choice.** Discuss how you choose books. In a literature-rich classroom, children will soon learn what proficient readers know and will be able to choose books based on:

    a. Friend's recommendations (provide time in class for book talks and sharing, which are different from book reports)

    b. Favorite author

    c. Genre

    d. Reading level (looking at text and reading the first page or two)

    e. Interest (Even difficult text is easier if the reader has a passion for the topic. Count how many first-grade boys can read words like *Tyrannosaurus Rex* and *Brachiosaurus*.)

Reading Logs

When children take charge of their reading, they act like readers; they do what real readers do. Students can begin to see themselves as readers by keeping a reading log, a list in which children record the titles, authors, illustrators, and perhaps genres of books read. Simple lists of books can provide data to identify the reader's interests and help teachers makes suggestions about other books and authors. These lists serve as a reminder to both teacher and children that we learn to read by reading. For example, the reading log (see Figure 2–3) compiled by a ten-year-old struggling reader is proof enough to her that she can read. Included on the list are not only books read independently, but also those read as a shared reading with a group or class, and books that were partner read or read in literature circles. All these book experiences belong to the children and the stories are now theirs. As the list grows, so does their impression of themselves as readers, as members of the "literacy club," as Frank Smith (1988) terms it.

Periodically reviewing logs can reveal the type of evidence of reading development that can be observed over time. Reading logs provide hard evidence that can be shared with parents and that students can use to articulate their strengths, reflect on their growth, and set goals for further learning. Many parents and students themselves are amazed at the sheer volume of reading that takes place over a few months' time in literature-based classrooms.

Reading journals or response journals require a response to the reading rather than just a listing of books read. Journals are discussed in Chapter 6.

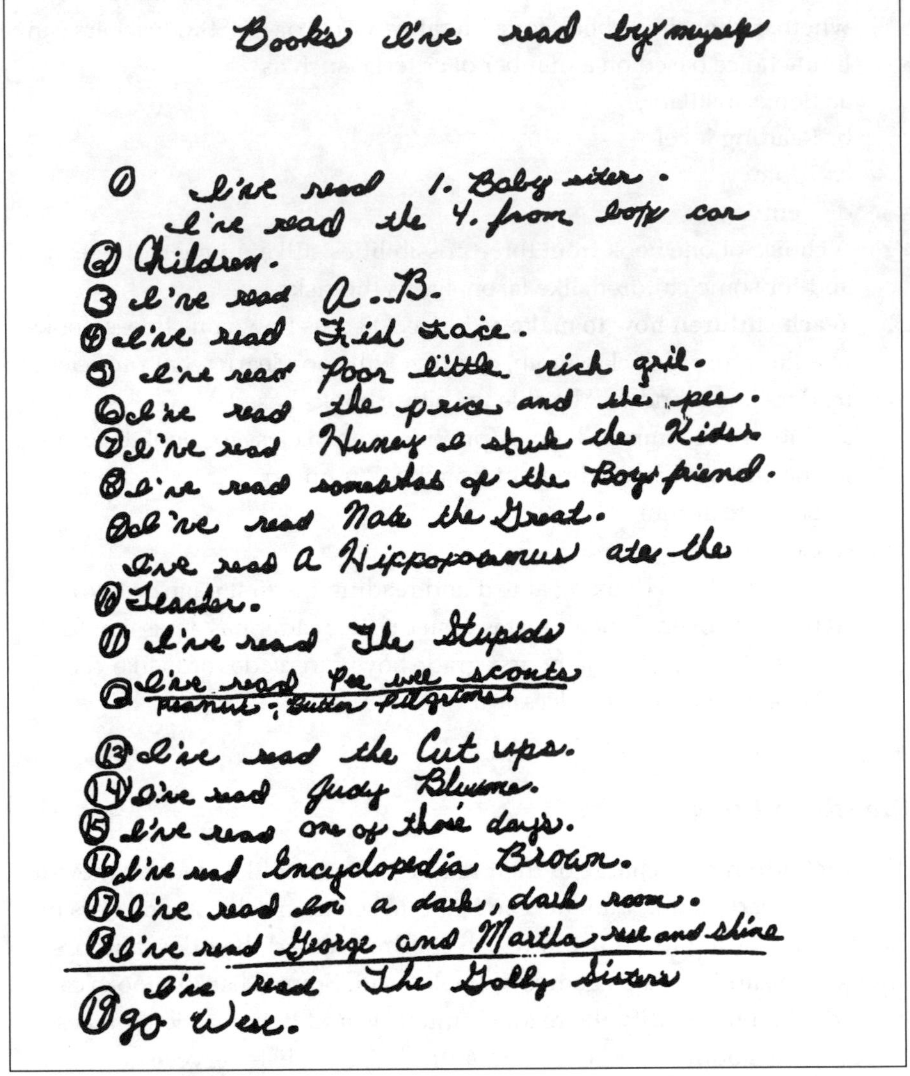

Books I've read by myself

(1) I've read 1. Baby siter.
I've read the 4. from boxcar
(2) Children.
(3) I've read A..B.
(4) I've read First race.
(5) I've read Poor little rich gril.
(6) I've read the price and the pee.
(7) I've read Harvey a stuck the Kider
(8) I've read somethas of the Boy friend.
(9) I've read Nate the Great.
I've read A Hippopotamus ate the
(10) Teacher.
(11) I've read The Stupids
(12) I've read Pee wee scouts
Peanut; Butter Pilgrimst
(13) I've read the Cut ups.
(14) I've read Judy Blume.
(15) I've read one of those days.
(16) I've read Encyclopedia Brown.
(17) I've read In a dark, dark room.
(18) I've read George and Martha rise and shine
I've read The Golly Sisters
(19) go West.

Figure 2–3 A ten-year-old's reading log

Beware of Reading as Competition

Reading logs need to be meaningful to students. To be productive, teachers must encourage and put value on independent reading; that is, independent reading must be seen as *worth* something because the teacher provides time for it, counts it in grading considerations, and respects student choice. Some teachers ask students to bring their reading logs to class once a week to share thoughts and reactions with classmates about their independent readings. Sharing helps readers feel part of a reading community, and the lists have a purpose beyond their use for the teacher. However, students can become competitive, comparing numbers of chapters or books read, so teachers need to downplay the number-of-books-read aspect and emphasize the reading process and responding to different books chosen. Competitiveness is a real danger when schools participate in special programs in which students receive prizes, such as pizza, for reading a certain number of books. We agree that reading should be celebrated and that eating pizza is fun, but competition doesn't belong in a reading curriculum. One student, Natalie, confided to us that she remembers using information gleaned from the back of the book and inside its jacket to qualify for a pizza. These programs foster not only competition, but might encourage students to choose books based on how quickly they can be read (to accumulate the required number of points) rather than according to genuine interest or appropriate reading level. For example, the way points are awarded in a contest might determine whether a reader chooses five short books instead of one long, classic work. Natalie was only slightly embarrassed by her back-of-the-book subterfuge because she saw the program as a game rather than as reading for meaning. Reading is not a contest, and published programs, such as Accelerated Reader, that make it one, can give students the wrong message about reading. The same caution applies to well-meaning principals and supervisors who challenge students in their schools to read an extraordinary number of books, and in return, the administrator will make a fool of himself (or herself) by dressing in a clown costume and taking pies in the face. Teachers should always remember why we read; it's not to accumulate points, to win pizzas, or even to advance to the next level after answering questions. Real readers read to enjoy, to learn, and to share ideas. Classrooms that celebrated this are classrooms of readers.

Sustained Silent Reading

In order to grow as readers, students need both the time and the opportunities to read in ways proficient readers deal with text. Reading instruction through direct teaching such as guided reading is important as is reading aloud to children, but students also need time to behave as real readers. Such opportunities not only develop skills, but also develop feelings of comfort and success as readers.

Classroom time devoted to silent independent reading is known by many acronyms—SSR (Sustained Silent Reading), DEAR (Drop Everything And Read), SQUIRT (Super Quiet Uninterrupted Independent Reading Time) to name a few. The length of time provided depends on age and development, but SSR can begin at five minutes a day for primary grades in September and extend to twenty minutes each day by the end of the school year. Older children who have had experience with SSR can begin at fifteen minutes per day and build up to thirty minutes a day as the year progresses.

Although not all agree, I still think it's quite important for the teacher to also read during SSR. This not only models reading, but also demonstrates to the children the teacher's belief in the importance of the activity. Everyone in the classroom, including aides, student teachers, visiting parents, should be reading during SSR.

Some teachers report that struggling readers often get off task during SSR. This is understandable since at this point in their reading development, independent reading is not necessarily much fun. Teachers need to support these students so they can feel successful during SSR. Some suggestions include:

1. **Help with choice ahead of time.** Often struggling readers choose a book that is too difficult, then give up after a couple of minutes, and feel that sense of failure. Help the child choose three or four appropriate possibilities every few days or every week (depending on age and length). (See Interest and Choice, earlier in this chapter.)

2. **Accept various reading texts.** Some children see books as overwhelming but will agree to try magazines, such as *Ranger Rick* or National Geographic's *World*. Try to compromise by agreeing that students will alternate one book with one magazine. Remember, the computer also offers some alternatives to traditional books, and reluctant readers will often read about Clifford or Arthur on the computer but not in a book.

3. **Adjust time accordingly.** Some students can read longer than others.

4. **Make the experience a comfortable one.** Students can see this time as a privilege, sitting on mats on the floor, under tables, in reading lofts, couches, and so on. (I seldom read for pleasure in a straight-backed chair at my desk.)

5. **Be available to help.** Make sure rules of SSR are clear and reasonable and students know why these rules are important. Provide alternatives for students who find they are stuck with a book they can't read or they don't enjoy. Provide support (reading partner, adult) to those who need extensive assistance.

6. **Provide time for sharing.** This is what proficient readers do. Children will want to make recommendations and such enthusiasm is contagious. It is also important for you to share your likes and dislikes. Young readers need to know that we also make adjustments in our choices based on interest and connections with the text.

7. **Provide plenty of reading material and choices.** Each classroom must have a library that provides books of varying reading levels, interests, and genres—nonfiction as well as fiction.

News and Announcement Charts

An authentic way to start the day with literacy is to create a news and announcement chart. Before the children enter the classroom in the morning, the teacher writes the day's news and any appropriate announcements the children should be aware of (on the chalkboard or on a flip chart or an easel). Then the news and announcements are posted and students see them when they come in.

Amy Walker, a teacher in western Pennsylvania, uses the same format for her chart each day. She always begins by writing a greeting, such as "Good Morning," and follows that with the day of the week and the date. She then lists the "specials," such as art or music, that are scheduled for the day, and perhaps follows this news with an activity planned for the day or one or two sentences about a book that is being shared as a class reading. Her news and announcements chart closes with a positive statement, such as "Have a happy and productive day." Amy deliberately keeps the language in the chart repetitive so the pattern becomes predictable. Such predictable exercises foster fluency and help students recognize words while they are reading. Some teachers encourage interaction by asking students to respond in some way on the chart. For example, the teacher may ask for a lunch tally on the chart, and the children would respond by checking under the appropriate column to indicate if they are buying a lunch or if they are only buying milk.

Such charts, once children get used to the predictability, encourage them in a natural way to take risks and to help one another. Sometimes the news and announcement chart serves as a springboard for discussing reading strategies or figuring out new words.

A variation of the news and announcement chart is morning news, which is written together as a shared writing activity. The teacher, using a predictable pattern, actually writes the morning news messages with the children the first thing each morning and offers two or three students each day a chance to share a part of their life as part of morning news. For example, after writing, "Good morning. Today is Tuesday, December 20 and we have music today," the teacher might call on Derek, who contributes the next sentence: "Yesterday I went Christmas shopping with my grandmother. We bought my mom's present." Susan might be the next volunteer who says, "I wrote a letter to Santa. I asked for computer games." The teacher would write the sentences down, pausing when appropriate to ask questions of the children to make the writing interactive. For example, before writing she might ask, "How do I begin the word *Christmas*?" hoping the children will remember to capitalize proper names. When writing "grandmother" she might ask what two words we see in the word *grandmother*. The teacher might even introduce the apostrophe since it makes sense to do so in this context.

After writing the morning news, the children read it again together, and sometimes volunteers can each read a sentence independently as the teacher sweeps her finger under the text.

Reading Buddies (Partner Reading)

Reading with a partner is a common practice in primary classrooms. Two children read a book together and respond to it through talking or writing. Depending on the age of the readers, or the reading development, this activity can take from ten to thirty minutes to complete.

There are several variations to partner reading but all emphasize meaning making and supporting developing readers. The technique is nonthreatening and helps children learn from each other; however, as with most successful student-led activities, partner reading must first be modeled and structured so students can successfully support one another. Teachers must:

1. **Set up the environment.** Students must feel safe taking risks and experimenting. Help children recognize and respect the fact that all learners have strengths and needs and we can support each other as we grow.
2. **Provide instruction.** Begin by discussing ways readers can support one another. Teachers can facilitate discussions by asking questions such as:
   a. What can we do when our buddy gets stuck on a word?
   b. When is it important to read every word exactly as it is written? For

instance, if your buddy says, "The boy rode past his home" instead of "The boy rode past his house" would we need to stop our buddy and correct the word? Why or why not?

c. When do you tell your buddy a word he or she doesn't know?
d. How can we talk about the story?
e. What if your buddy doesn't remember something in the story that you think is important?

As teachers and students discuss these questions, responses can be recorded and a wall chart can be constructed from responses with specific ideas for buddy reading procedures.

3. **Choose texts and formats**. There is no one format for buddy reading. Often two readers read the same book, taking turns reading aloud. This book can be selected by the teacher or student. The turn-taking can be every other page, or reader one reading the first half of the book and reader two reading the second half. Either way is successful with some readers and the choice depends on the readers themselves and/or the text being read.

Another format is each reader selecting a book (or being assigned a book or story by the teacher) and the first child reading her book aloud to her buddy on day one. The next session, the second child reads his book aloud to his buddy. After each reading, time is allotted for discussion and connections. Older readers may want to read their books silently and retell their books to their buddies, answering questions and responding to comments.

Very young children may benefit from reading aloud in unison. This is often helpful to the struggling readers when paired with a reader who is having less difficulty. What results is sometimes a type of echo reading and readers might be encouraged to reread the text until the reading becomes more fluent.

Buddy or partner reading can be used for a variety of purposes and can utilize writing, drawing, or talking. Gretchen Owocki (2003) provides ideas for various partner strategy explorations in Figure 2–4.

Reading to Younger Readers

Children of all ages need to see themselves as readers. As my granddaughter Brooke rides in the car and reads environmental print, such as the McDonald's signs or the stop sign, or reads "To Brooke from Santa" on Christmas gifts, my daughter responds, "Good reading, Brooke." At four years old, my granddaughter knows she is a reader and is interested in adding to the repertoire of text that she reads both independently and with another, more advance reader. Her older brother Ryan, who is six, often helps Brooke with more advanced text when he reads signs along the roadside, such as "Bridge May Be Icy." He also reads *The Cat in the Hat* at bedtime and Brooke loves to chime in when she knows a rhyming word.

Developing readers must see themselves as readers. Even struggling

Partner Strategy Explorations	
Strategy	Depending on what is appropriate, partners may engage in the explorations by writing, drawing, or talking.
Predicting and Inferring	• Use the cover to predict what the book will be about (fiction) or to predict what you will learn (nonfiction). As you read, discuss whether your predictions are confirmed. • Do a picture walk to make some predictions about what will happen (fiction) or what you will learn (nonfiction). As you read, discuss whether your predictions are confirmed. • Make an inference based on the cover of the book. As you read, discuss whether your inference is confirmed. • Make an inference about a character/personality.
Purpose Setting	• Do a picture walk to set a purpose for reading. • Decide together on a purpose for reading. After reading, tell how your goals/purposes/hopes were met or not met. • With nonfiction, create a KWL chart or a gathering information from text chart. • With fiction, use a story map to focus on and discuss key story elements.
Retelling	• Stop after every few pages to summarize what has happened so far or what you have learned so far. • After reading, synthesize what you have read. • After reading, retell the problem-resolution sequence and tell what you think about it. • After reading, create a story map and use it to retell what you have read. • After reading, use a checklist to retell what you have read. • During and after reading, create an informational text organizer. Use it to retell.
Questioning	• Use sticky notes to record questions you have while reading. • After every three pages, ask your partner a question. • During reading, stop to tell what you wonder about. • After reading, develop a question for the author.
Monitoring	• After every few pages, stop to summarize what you have just read. • After every few pages, tell one thing you have learned. • Stop to talk about words or ideas that confuse you. • Choose three words that you both find interesting. • Find a word that is new to both of you. • Make a record of important or confusing words. • Use sticky notes to code the text together.

Figure 2–4 Ideas for various partner strategy explorations

Visualizing	• During or after reading, draw or tell how you picture a key character or personality. • During or after reading, draw or tell how you picture the setting. • Choose a picture and reflect on what you might hear, see, smell, taste, and feel from the page. • Draw or write about an image you had while reading. Include as many details as possible. • Choose any section of text not pictured and describe your mental image.
Connecting	• As you read, use a sticky note to mark something that the text reminds you of (a personal connection). Discuss your connection after reading. • As you read, tell about things that surprise you or are new to you. • As you read, stop to talk about things that interest you. • Discuss a between-text connection. • Draw a picture of one character or personality with whom you particularly identified. Compare pictures with your partner. • Discuss a connection between something you've read and something you already knew.
Deciding What's Important	• As you read, stop to discuss the main ideas. • After reading, create a diagram, picture, or model that shows what you have learned. • Choose an important quote or picture. Discuss why it is important. • Create an ideas and details chart. • Create a time line. • Use sticky notes to mark interesting text features.
Evaluating	• Decide together on an event you find interesting and discuss what makes it interesting. • Find an interesting illustration and discuss what makes it interesting. • Tell about a favorite part or a part you didn't like (tell why). • Tell about a favorite character or a character you didn't like (tell why). • Retell what the main character/personality did and what you would do in a similar situation (tell why). • Decide together on an alternative to the resolution. • Tell what you think about the illustrations (tell why). • Decide on key ways you will use the information you read about. • Discuss why you think the author wrote this text. • Discuss who you think should read this text (tell why). • Discuss how you feel about the author's use of language (tell why).

Figure 2–4 continued

readers can read some text and often, with practice, can share their expertise with younger readers. This is also an appropriate way of providing an authentic rereading experience. Asking a third grader to read *We're Going on a Bear Hunt* to first graders or kindergarteners gives the third grader a reason for practicing a text at his reading level, but one that is too "young" for him. Asking him to help the younger readers gives him an opportunity to practice text at a level commensurate with his development so he can feel accomplished and like an "expert" as he reads it aloud to younger children (something that doesn't happen often in his third-grade classroom).

Another strategy that helps all readers involved is matching third graders with kindergarten or first grader reading buddies. Once a week, the third graders can support the younger readers and every third grader can see him- or herself as an accomplished reader. The teachers must help the third graders learn appropriate ways of supporting their younger buddies by providing strategies and activities that will be helpful and interesting. (See the previous section, Reading Buddies.)

Owning Books

It is important for all readers to own their own books. A friend of mine, Amy Walker, has been a special education teacher for many years and has helped instill a love of reading in many struggling readers. She knows the power books can have in her students' lives. One of her former students, Brad, was an unusual student, even in a class of adolescents with the label "emotionally disturbed." He was a walking demolition man, destroying everything he touched. He ripped his clothes, broke games, snapped all his pencils, and literally destroyed everything he came into contact with. Even with counseling and therapy, he treated everything with distain.

During the course of the school year, Amy gave Brad his own copy of S. E. Hinton's book *The Outsiders*, which the class had read together. For weeks, Brad carried that book around with him and it remained in perfect condition, although it was obviously being read. Finally Amy asked, "Brad, how come nothing's happened to the book?" He looked at her and answered simply, "No one ever gave me anything that was worth anything before."

Books are precious possessions and every child has a right to own them. Many children are fortunate enough to have hundreds, but there are many who have never owned any or at best one or two. There are ways we can at least help get books not only into children's hands but home in their rooms on a special shelf. Sometimes classrooms order books through book clubs and the points earned can be used for free books that the teacher distributes on birthdays or other holidays. This is not practical, however, in poorer school districts where parents don't have money to buy books, even through these discount clubs. Teachers can add to their class libraries by purchasing books at garage sales, and they can sometimes find help through small grants awarded by large retail stores such as Target or Wal-Mart (see specific store websites for information). Other sources of help can be parent organizations, local churches, community groups, and so on. The education students at Slippery Rock University of Pennsylvania organized a book drive asking the university community of students, faculty, and staff for donations of new or gently read children's books and set up donation boxes around the campus. The books were donated to a neighboring school district and distributed to children, many of whom had few books to call their own.

In addition to owning personal copies of books, children can have a sense of ownership through the community library. When possible, teachers should make sure all children have library cards and make the case that a field trip to the public library is much more valuable than one to an amusement park. We need to open the world to all children and the way to do it is to get books into their lives and their hands.

Environmental Print

It's important for children of all ages to "read the world." This can be done in many natural ways as part of a day and in situations that are appropriate and help children see themselves as readers. Although as adults we can encourage reading in everyday ways—signs, ads, print in stores—as teachers we can bring environmental print into the classroom and value it so children will see that this too is reading.

It's easy to make environmental print books to keep on classroom shelves to encourage beginning readers to not only read these books but to recognize that they are capable of reading.

Begin by cutting out box fronts (cereal boxes, toothpaste cartons, macaroni and cheese, rice, crackers, cake mix, potato chips). These can be mounted on eight-and-a-half-by-eleven-inch–paper, laminated and bound into a book with an appropriate title, such as "Things I Buy in a Grocery Store." Other books can be made that connect print children see in the world to the world of literacy. For example, a book called "Road Signs" can include signs drawn or cut out from a driver's manual and enlarged, mounted, and laminated, or one called "Foods I Like to Eat" can be created with advertisements for favorite foods cut from magazines or newspaper ads. The same magazines and newspapers could produce a book called "Places I Like to Visit" with local attractions such as the zoo, nature parks, amusement parks, bowling, theme restaurants, and other localities that children would recognize.

Another common but somewhat less authentic method of encouraging reading of the world is to label items and encourage the children to "read the room." Labels can be put on the desk, flag, doors, cubbies, pencil boxes, crayons, windows, plants, centers (writing center, reading center, play center), sink, bathroom, paper, and so on. Seeing these common words will help young children understand the concept of a word unit and many will begin to use these words in their writing.

Encouraging the use of reading in everyday activities also helps to teach reading outside of the typical reading lesson. Going over the calendar and weather daily, looking at connected words such as the name of the month or day of the week and weather terms such as *cloudy, sunny, cold,* and *windy,* can provide a wealth of daily literacy teaching opportunities. Reading the lunch menu with the children on a daily basis is also a natural reading lesson.

Literacy Play Boxes

Helping children notice print in the world not only sets a purpose for reading, but connects two aspects of a child's world—the world of play (pretend) and the world of adults. Children go to the grocery store and play store at home and school; they go to fast food restaurants and play McDonald's on their own. This pretend play not only supports imaginative development and social interaction, but it can also naturally support literacy development.

Teachers can support this sort of activity by putting together literacy play boxes (Morrow 1989). Some schools enlist the help of parent or PTO members to put together the play boxes that have the components needed for various play activities. For instance, in the Restaurant box, the children might find menus (often placemats donated by nearby restaurants that print children's menu choices), hats, bags, plastic play food (such as hamburgers, fries, catsup, milk, hot dogs), order pads, receipt pads for the bill, pencils, and play money. While the children are using the props in the box to play restaurant, they will be using reading and writing in appropriate real-world situations.

Other literacy boxes could include Doctor's Office, Shoe Store, Gas Station, Bookstore, Veterinarian. For example, the Shoe Store play box might hold some sort of instrument to measure feet (donated by a shoe store or fashioned by a parent so children can match their footprint with the sizes), boxes with size and style on the ends, receipt pads and pencils, and a shoe catalogue. The Doctor's Office play box might contain prescription pads, pencils, first aid supplies, stethoscope, reflex hammer, medical book, and patient charts to write diagnoses.

Explaining the purpose of literacy play boxes to parents and enlisting their support will generate other ideas and materials for the boxes. Teachers should remember to emphasize the reading/writing connections and the literacy that this sort of pretend playing supports.

Interactive Reading

Many times younger, less experienced readers benefit from interactive reading experiences with an adult. During such times, the adult reader reads to the child with enthusiasm and expression but provides opportunities throughout the reading for the child to participate. Rebus stories are the most common of these interactive experiences in which the adult reads the text and the child chimes in when there is a picture to represent a word. For example:

The was shining and there was not a 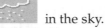 in the sky.

These texts are particularly helpful in demonstrating the concept of a word unit and it helps if the adult is pointing to the text as it is being read. This also helps young readers read to make sense, one of the most important first steps in learning to read independently.

There are other ways to make reading an interactive experience. Leaving out words and having the child read them by using context and picture clues also helps them stay involved in the story and actively participate. The strategy works one on one, but it is also successful during group reading or shared reading, especially when Big Books are used so the entire group can read the text.

CHAPTER THREE

Phonemic Awareness and Phonics

Two Approaches to Phonics

If one listened to television commercials or federal mandates, one would assume that the key to reading is phonics, yet it is important to note that there are actually two major approaches to phonics instruction: synthetic and analytic.

The synthetic approach to phonics instruction, although popular, has little to do with actual oral language. When teaching with this approach, the teacher first instructs children in the relationship between letters and their sounds. This is usually done through drill and practice with techniques such as the letter of the day, alphabet people, and flashcards. Following the learning of letter sounds, children are taught to segment and blend practicing the individual letter sounds in words. *Cat* would be segmented into three sounds, k-ă-tə (this is quite difficult to do auditorally, since in oral language we do not segment this word into three sounds, but actually two sounds, k-at). When blending, teachers encourage children to blend discrete sounds into words, for instance: da-o-ga blended to become dog. (Unfortunately, since oral language does not lend itself to this synthetic approach, when asking children to blend da-o-ga, what results is often no word at all, but a series of isolated sounds.)

The analytic approach to phonics instruction uses what we know about oral language to help decode words. Sight words are taught through repetition and practice using techniques such as words walls and word banks drawn from authentic reading situations (see Chapter 4). Decoding is taught in the context of meaningful reading, and while meaning is always the paramount purpose for reading, teachers help students to see similarities between words, patterns, onset and rime, words within words, prefixes, suffixes, and so on (discussed later in this chapter and in Chapter 4). Although when teaching at the word level, "the process may be broken down to examine individual pieces, before the instruction ends, the process should be put back together so that children see the relationship between the part and the whole," Bill Harp (1989) reminds us.

Importance of Phonics

No one would argue that phonics isn't important in reading and reading instruction. Good readers use all three cueing systems, of which graphic cues are one, but what must be remembered is that learning phonics is not a precursor to learning to read. Actually, phonics should be taught in the context of authentic reading situations.

The same premise holds true for phonemic awareness (discussed later in this chapter). For young children, listening for sounds in words, recognizing letter and sound connections, and rhyming can be fun and such language play can be helpful to developing readers, but along with such play should be real reading situations, handling books, choosing books, listening to stories being read, talking about stories, and noticing literacy in everyday life (environmental print).

Onsets and Rime

Books and charts with rhyme and repetition are often used during shared and guided reading, and children enjoy the rhythm of the language in such books. Teachers must remember that, although these books are wonderful for skills lessons in phonics, readers don't read for that purpose. If the story has a story line, no matter how simple, it is important to attend to meaning first, modeling the purpose of reading for children. After attending to meaning, it is appropriate to use the language in the book to reinforce what children know about how language works. (Some books, however, are written for the sheer joy of language and have little story line. Well-known examples of this type of book are the many Dr. Seuss books that children enjoy for the playfulness of the text.) After reading a book with a rhyming pattern, and attending to the story, it is helpful to use the text to help the children recognize the rhyming patterns and see how words are similar. Knowing how to read one word helps them read a similar one, especially if looked at in context. An example would be: "The *cat* in the *hat*."

As children identify rhyming words, the words can be put on index cards and put in a pocket chart. Help the children see how words that rhyme have the same pattern or are in the same spelling family. The ending pattern (rime) can be underlined in each word by the teacher and the children can see how changing the initial consonant (onset) makes a new word. For example, the *-at* rime can be combined with various onsets— beginning consonants *c, h, m, s, b, f: hat, cat, mat, sat, bat, fat*. Figure 3–1 shows a list of words from *The Cat in the Hat*.

hat	hear	play	ball	sit	bump	pot	tricks	sunny
cat	near	day	all	it	jump	not	kicks	funny
mat	*clear	say	fall	bit	*lump	jot	*licks	*bunny
sat	*dear	away	wall	lit	*stump	*rot	*sticks	[honey]
that	*fear	way	hall	hit	*hump	*got	*picks	[money]
pat		*lay	tall	*fit	*clump	*hot		
*bat	shame	*hay	*call	*spit			fan	
*rat	game	*pay	*mall	*split	net	now	man	
*fat	*lame	*ray		*mit	bet	bow	*can	
*chat	*came		hook	*pit	yet	*sow	*pan	
	*same	wish	look		*set	*cow	*ran	
	*blame	fish	*nook	out	*get	*wow	*Dan	
	*tame	dish	*took	about	*let		*tan	
			*shook	*shout	*jet		*van	
				*stout			*Jan	

The asterisked words are examples of other rimes that can be added to those from the book. The bracketed words have the same sound but different rime.

Figure 3–1 Onsets and rimes from *The Cat in the Hat*

After using the words from the story, the teacher and children can come up with other words that fit the pattern. Sometimes it is best for teachers to have possibilities ready, since the English spelling system is irregular and dialects vary, and some words that may seem to fit the pattern actually do not. This needs to be pointed out to children in the context of reading, when there are other cues, syntax, and semantics that will help them decode these irregular words (for example, *box* and *locks*, *may* and *weigh*). Onset and rime is often referred to as spelling patterns and a list of the thirty-seven most common rimes can be found in Appendix A.

Tongue Twisters

Tongue twisters are fun for children as well as for adults, and they are an enjoyable way to reinforce the sound of beginning consonants. Some traditional favorites serve as wonderful chants on the playground to call out while swinging, jumping rope, or bouncing balls. Who doesn't remember this tongue twister:

> She sells seashells
> Down by the seashore.

Or these:

> Peter Piper picked a peck of pickled peppers.
> How many pecks of pickled peppers did Peter Piper pick?

> How much wood would a woodchuck chuck
> If a woodchuck could chuck wood?

Children can make up their own tongue twisters using their own or friends' names in the pattern of a popular 1960s song, "The Name Game":

> Peter, Peter
> Bo Beater
> Banana Banna Foe Feater
> Fee Fi Moe Meater
> Peter

Or:

> Jim, Jim
> Bo Bim
> Banana Banna Foe Fim
> Fee Fi Moe Mim
> Jim

Another simple way of making up tongue twisters using children's names is by taking the sound of the first letter in the name and using it over and over in each sentence. The names could be taken in alphabetical order, if the teacher wanted to emphasize the letters of the alphabet, but it isn't necessary. For example:

Brooke brought bright blue berries to breakfast.

Courtney catches cute cats in the cornfield.

Donna dances around dandelions with delight.

Jeff jumped over jelly jars.

Laura looked lovely in lavender lace.

Patty picked purple pansies.

Mom met Matt at the Monroe mall.

Ryan ran rapidly after the racing rabbits.

Phonemic Awareness

When we speak of phonemic awareness, we are generally concerned with helping students hear the individual sounds in our language and understand that sounds can be written down, represented by letters and various combinations of letters.

A *phoneme* is the smallest sound unit that can be represented in written language. In oral language, we are not aware of these smallest units since we talk in words and sentences to make meaning. Children do become aware of sounds as they learn to read (but not as a *precursor* to reading). One of the first ways we can assess children's awareness of speech sounds is to look at their invented spellings and the link they make between sounds and letters (see the discussion of writing later in this chapter).

Letter Recognition

Letter recognition, recognizing and naming letters of the alphabet and understanding that letters make specific sounds, has long been seen as having a high correlation with reading, specifically success in reading in first grade (Durrell 1958). However, research also indicates that teaching children to recognize letters of the alphabet does not necessarily help them learn to read (Ohnmact 1969; Samuels 1972). Knowing letters in pre-kindergarten or in kindergarten is probably a result of interest kindled at home or in preschool programs. Even television shows such as Sesame Street have helped many children become aware of letters and learn to differentiate between the letters of the alphabet.

However, in the United States, there is a great emphasis on letter recognition in primary grades and often children are assessed on their ability to name individual letters. For this reason, kindergarten teachers must find ways to teach the letters of the alphabet that are interesting and, what is more important, authentic. Instruction can be woven into classroom routines and activities and letter recognition should be taught not in isolation, but in meaningful language contexts. Some suggestions for teaching letter recognition include:

1. **Letters in children's names**. Using the children's names is a great way to begin teaching children about letters. Students' own names and the names their friends are of great interest to them, so children's names should be prominently displayed in the classroom. Counting letters in each name, discussing the first letter, and tracing names using shaving cream or sand as a kindergarten activity is of interest to some children. Using this information in everyday activities makes this practice fun and authentic. For example, teachers may say, "Everyone whose name begins with the letter *B*, and sounds like ba-ba, please line up for recess. Thank you, Brandon, Bobby, and Billy. Next, those whose names begin with *M*, and sounds like mm-mm. Whose names begin with *M*? Yes, Madison, Mike, and Melissa."

Names can also be used for minilessons looking for similar letters, lengths of names, and repeating letters.

2. **Alphabet books**. There are wonderful alphabet books from themed approaches such as *Eating the Alphabet: Fruits and Vegetables from A to Z* by Lois Ehlert to whimsical ones like *Chick A Chick A Boom Boom* by Bill Martin, Jr. and John Archambault. Preschool, kindergarten, and first-grade classes should have a variety of such books for children to read on their own or with others. One of my favorite books that combines learning the alphabet with a story line is a Toby book, *Toby's Alphabet Walk* by Cyndy Szekeres.

Children can also make their own alphabet books (see Appendix B for book-making ideas or more elaborate directions on the Internet at *www.pgcps.pg.k12.md.us/~univpark/bookbinding.html*). Each child can choose a letter, illustrate it with words that begin with the chosen letter, and write about it. The pages can be xeroxed and stapled, so each child can have a copy of a class alphabet book.

3. **Letters in context of real reading**. When writing a language experience story, invite children to pay attention to individual letters as you write. Morning message or lessons using Big Books are natural ways to notice letters (see News and Announcements Charts in Chapter 2).

4. **Letter detective**. Choose a letter to investigate. Unlike a letter a week, students can choose a letter to investigate, to search for on food boxes, signs, in magazines, and in other sources of print (for example: *w* in Wheaties, Wendy's, wagon, Wonder bread, and William). Children can make books about the letters they investigate. (All twenty-six letters are not necessary; some children may choose to investigate one or two letters, others eight or ten letters.) Children often choose letters in their names and other "important" letters, such as *s, r, t, a*, and *m*.

5. **Letters in writing**. As children emerge as writers, it is important that they have real reasons to write and that their writing development is respected. Whether children are scribble writing, using mock letters or more conventional attempts at print, their writing should be valued, read, and displayed. Many children will use individual letters to stand for words and will experiment with other ways to use letters in their writing. (See Appendix C.)

6. **Alphabet blocks and magnetic letters.** Simply putting magnetic letters on the chalkboard where little hands can reach them encourages play such as lining up the letters in order as the alphabet is sung or chanted or writing of names using the letters. The same type of play is possible with alphabet blocks.

Finding Little Words in Bigger Words

It is important for children to use strategies for figuring out unknown words rather than always sounding out. Proficient readers know to look for what they know in an unknown word. This can be demonstrated in minilessons as such words show up in stories or text (such as news and announcement chart, lunch menu, and so on). It is important to remind children that using all clues are important—how the word is used in the sentence, what makes sense, and how the word looks.

For example, a line in a story might read, "The yellow *kitten* sat on the steps looking at me." I tell the children that although I am not sure of the word *kitten*, I first skip it and think of what makes sense. I know it is something small and yellow with eyes and can sit on steps, so I think it can be an animal, a toy, or a child dressed in yellow. But if I look at the word I can take the clues I already know about the meaning in the sentence and try to see what I know about the word. (See Think-Alouds in Chapter 7.)

I use the letters in my pocket chart and spell out the word *k-i-t-t-e-n* and ask myself, "What words do I know that are in this word?" and I immediately come up with three:

kit

it

ten

(I don't scramble the letters; I want the children to see that I need to use "chunks" of the word.) I know, looking at the small word, that the word is really two smaller words put together, and I figure out that what is small and yellow and sitting is a *kit-ten*.

I use this same lesson over and over as it makes sense, in morning message, when postteaching vocabulary or when difficult words are going to appear in a story. Teaching this as a think-aloud also demonstrates over and over what a proficient reader does. This teaches children to be strategic readers.

Riddles and Rhymes

Helping children play with words, but doing so in a context, helps them to use more than one cueing system to figure out words. Riddles, such as the ones that follow, require the students to use meaning, but they also help them understand the concept of rhyme. Telling kids that rhyming words have the same sounds can sometimes be quite unclear. For instance, one second grader who was having trouble with the concept of rhyming told the teacher that the word *walk* rhymed with the word *work* because "they sound the same." Obviously, he had listened to the lessons on rhyming but was now quite confused. The boy needed to move on and not be caught up in the idea of rhyming for the sake of rhyming. Since the reason for employing knowledge of rhyming is learning phonemic similarities, tests and curriculum that supposedly assess phonemic awareness by rhyming words outside of context put unnecessary pressure on learners. Riddles help kids put this activity into a proper perspective and take away some of the confusion.

Some examples of phonemic riddles would be:

I have in mind a word that rhymes with *far*. We ride in it. It is called a ____ (*car*).

I have in mind a word that rhymes with *tar*. It twinkles in the sky. It is a ____ (*star*).

I have in mind a word that rhymes with *keep*. I do it at night in my bed. I go to ____ (*sleep*).

I have in mind a word that rhymes with *rest*. This is a direction; it's not north, south, east, but ____ (*west*).

I have in mind a word that rhymes with *sticks*. My dog is smart. I teach him new ____ (*tricks*).

I have in mind a word that rhymes with *me*. I sit under it when it is hot. It is a ____ (*tree*).

The words can be displayed in the pocket chart for the children to choose from and then paired so the students can discuss the similarities.

Nursery Rhymes

Phonemic awareness is best developed naturally rather than taught through worksheets and drills. If we provide time in our classrooms for children to hear rhyme, they will learn to enjoy language and learn how it works. Many children come to school with a background of nursery rhymes and songs, but many do not. Kindergarten and first grade are times when all children will benefit from learning and enjoying rhymes that train their ear to listen to language. Just reciting familiar rhymes during the day help children enjoy the sound of language but also increase their awareness of sound. If possible, books, charts, and posters that reinforce what they hear in print can also be displayed.

Poems in the lunch line, on the playground, and while waiting for a visitor not only fill the time but also provide a lesson in phonemic awareness in a natural, enjoyable way. A new series of poetry books by Gay Su Pinnell and Irene Fountas (2004) offers a myriad of ideas and possibilities.

My favorite poem at playground time is "The Swing" by Robert Louis Stevenson (all my nieces and grandchildren join in shouting the word in parentheses as they swing):

> How do you like to go up in a swing?
> Up in the air so blue?
> Oh, I do think it's the pleasantest thing,
> Ever a child can ____ (do)!
>
> Up in the air and over the wall,
> Till I can see so wide,
> Rivers and trees and cattle and all
> Over the country____ (side).
>
> Till I look down on the garden green,
> Down on the roof so brown—
> Up in the air I go flying again,
> Up in the air and ____ (down).

Another set of poems concerning weather can teach phonemic awareness.

> The rain is raining all around,
> It falls on field and tree,
> It rains on the umbrellas here,
> And on the ships at ____ (sea).
>
> **—Robert Louis Stevenson**

Rain, Rain go away,
Come again another ____ (day).
Rain, Rain go away,
Little (child's name or "children") want(s) to ____ (play).

Rhyming Books

There are so many wonderful rhyming books; it would be difficult to even begin to list them. Dr. Seuss provided us with "classics," such as *The Cat in the Hat* and *There's a Wocket in my Pocket*. Other books, such as *Jesse Bear, What Will You Wear?* by N. W. Cakstrom, use rhyme in a delightful, sensible way to connect the reading to children's lives. All children love the antics of the mischievous monkeys in *Five Little Monkeys* and love to recite it with motions while reading. Another funny favorite to use year-round is *Chicken Soup with Rice* by Maurice Sendak; a must for every classroom is a musical version by Carole King, sung by Gail Swain and friends.

No matter what rhyming book you choose to share with children, remember:

1. Books that are fun can become favorites that children want to hear and read over and over.
2. When children listen to a book more than once, you can explain that the book is fun because of the rhymes. Begin to stop at a rhyming word and let the child or children supply it for you.
3. Start listing the rhyming words on the board and see how they are the same and how they are different. For example the rhymes to be listed from *Five Little Monkeys* would be: *bed, head, said, bed.* Three endings that sound the same are written *-ed, -ead,* and *-aid.*

Counting Words in Speech—Matching Letters to Sounds

One of the first steps in reading is to understand the concept of *word*. This can be accomplished in a myriad of ways, one of the most important being the reading of whole texts and stories, sweeping a finger under the text so the child connects the written word with spoken language, showing that written words carry a message and have meaning. As part of the reading experience, parents and teachers can use simple techniques that help children hear words and start to see them as units (since this is difficult to do in spoken language; we speak quickly and blend words so it is difficult to hear them as separate units in speech).

We can use simple speech to help children understand that our language is made up of words. An enjoyable way to do this is through counting words in a game. Each child is given a paper cup with tokens, perhaps the sort used to play Bingo. The teacher begins by saying a simple sentence, like "Suzy has a lovely smile." After saying it normally, the teacher repeats the sentence, saying it slowly: "Suzy . . . has . . . a . . . lovely . . . smile." As the teacher says the sentence slowly, the children put a token down on their desks for each word in the sentence. Saying this sentence again, together, the children point to each token. As children get used to this activity, they can take turns making up sentences and saying them first normally and then slowly as their classmates place tokens on the desk or table as they count the words.

This activity is a simple and enjoyable way to help children begin to understand that sentences are made up of individual words. (It also helps with counting skills!)

Clapping Syllables

It is sometimes easier to hear syllables than to hear words in our language, and often beginning readers will separate word units into syllables as they read, thinking each syllable they hear is a word. If teachers begin with words children are familiar with, like their names, children begin to see that a single word can have more than one component. Saying the name "Danny," the teacher and students will clap twice, "Dan" (clap) "-ny" (clap). Saying the names of children, clapping or tapping, will be reinforced by the children's interest in rhythm and it will help to first call each syllable a "beat." After the children are comfortable with clapping first names, the teacher can add last names, like "Kath-leen Strick-land," and clap four times. Soon the children will begin to see that names that are shorter have fewer beats than longer names, so it is important to have the names written on the board or on a poster so they can make this association.

This game is also fun to use with animals (*horse, elephant, hippo, rabbit, ostrich,* and so on) or objects in the classroom (*desk, chalkboard, door, clock, window, flag, pencil,* and so on). After clapping once for the word *dog* and three times for the word *dinosaur,* show the two words to the children and have them guess which is which. "Since *dinosaur* takes three claps, it is probably the longer word."

The rhythm of clapping can also be used when reading books with rhyme, rhythm, and repetition, such as Bill Martin Jr.'s *Brown Bear, Brown Bear* and *Chick A Chick A Boom Boom.* As children clap the words as these books are read, they begin to make connections between the beats and the word units.

Segmenting Words—Sound Boxes

Even after much work with onsets and rime, many children have difficulty segmenting words. This is understandable because, as we've seen with our work with onsets and rimes (discussed earlier in this chapter), our spoken language does not naturally break down into phonemes. However, there are times when children must be able to segment words into phonemes, more so for testing purposes than for the purpose of reading. It is sometimes helpful to give students some practice in this segmenting into phonemes in a way that makes it less threatening and more fun.

A technique used often in Reading Recovery (Clay 1995) is sound boxes (Elkonin 1973). Children are given a drawing of three boxes and as they hear sounds in words, they put a token into a box.

The teacher or partner says a familiar word composed of three letters and three sounds, such as *cat, dog, mat,* and *box.* Often there are pictures available of these nouns and after seeing and saying the words, the children are encouraged to stretch the word (*c-c-c-a-a-a-t-t-t*) and to put a token in each box to represent each phoneme in the word. After some practice with three-letter words, use some four-letter words with three phonemes such as *four, duck,* and *lake* and use the three boxes again. Soon the children will be ready for four boxes and can stretch out words with four phonemes, like *nest, bank,* and *bird.*

One word of caution. Sound boxing is quite difficult to do when you cannot visualize the word and are relying only on sound. It is still an artificial way to look at language and not directly related to speech (see earlier discussion of the synthetic approach). If children are having extreme difficulty with this, do not let it interfere with real reading; concentrate on onset and rime, which will be more helpful and translate from speech to reading more efficiently and logically.

Alphabet Sound Word Examples

As children learn more letter–sound connections, they begin to associate certain words with their corresponding letter. Although published series often supply example words, these words sometimes confuse children because the associations aren't their own. For example, my granddaughter, Brooke, made up her own alphabet game that we play when driving in the car or waiting for our food at a restaurant. She always begins with *A* and says the sound and comes up with a word: "ah, ah apple." Then it's my turn to come up with an A-word. We don't start the next letter until everyone in the car or at the table contributes. Brooke has also found a way to give herself extra turns by having her stuffed bear or kitty that is with her get a turn. She offers Kitty's contribution in a different voice. The wonderful thing is that the words contributed aren't always the same. Teachers can create this kind of alphabet sound word play by making their own example chart with the children. For vowels and consonants with two sounds, I suggest identifying two words, one for each sound the letter makes. Here is an example of a chart one group of primary children came up with.

Sample Chart

Aa	apple, angel
Bb	banana
Cc	cookies, city
Dd	dog
Ee	egg, east
Ff	fish
Gg	gorilla, gymnastics
Hh	happy
Ii	ice cream, igloo
Jj	jump
Kk	Kelsey
Ll	letter
Mm	mosquito
Nn	Nemo
Oo	orange, oval
Pp	peanut
Qq	quack
Rr	rabbit
Ss	snake
Tt	Tigger
Uu	umbrella
Vv	valentine
Ww	wind
Xx	x-ray, xylophone
Yy	yard
Zz	zoo

Gathering All the Rhymes

Gathering all the rhymes is an activity that follows the reading of a text that contains many rhyming words. Read a story through once to appreciate the story and enjoy the sound and rhythm of the language. After the first reading, ask the children what made this book or story fun to read. Answers may include pictures, silly characters, and silly words or rhymes. Tell the students you're going to read each page again and their job will be to help you to gather up all the rhymes and put them on the board or in the pocket chart.

After reading *Turtle Time* by Sandol Stoddard, you would have the following sets of rhyming words:

play, day, away, say	is, his	see, me
hat, that	(head), bed, sled, Fred	find, behind
car, far	around, found	deep, sleep, keep
still, hill	ball, all, small	hand, understand
maps, naps	eat, treat	
inside, hide	cake, make	

The children could look at why the words rhyme and identify spelling patterns (or rimes).

Writing

Those in the profession recognize the importance of writing in the development of reading. Studies show that children actually write before they can read (see *Language Stories and Literacy Lessons* by Harste, Woodward, and Burke [1984]). The types of writing that are often seen as children experiment with written language are illustrated in Appendix C; as children make connections between letters and sounds they use this knowledge along with their illustrations to represent their thoughts and ideas in language, as seen in Figure 3–2. As awareness develops, usually by being read to, children recognize the ideas of a word unit and combine this with their understanding of letter–sound correspondence. It is at this time that *invented spelling* (or what is sometimes called *temporary spelling* for political correctness) enables a writer to use phonics as a way to put words together.

Stretching Words

This technque is one way to support children as they write independently. Stretching words is similar to segmenting, but like a rubber band stretching, the child says the word slowly, trying to pay attention to each individual sound in the word so it can be reproduced and read by readers as well as by the writer. *Playground* becomes pl-a-gr-ond and *summer* becomes s-a-m-r. Figure 3–3 illustrates seven-year-old Kelly's use of phonics as she stretches words like *aunt* and *Pennsylvania*. Encouraging such writing not only supports a child's phonetic ability, it empowers her as an independent writer who can share her ideas through her writing.

Figure 3–2 "See the Scac [skunk]"

Figure 3–3 Kelly writes about a trip to Pennsylvania to visit her aunt.

Invented Spelling

Invented spelling progresses and changes as the child has more experience with written text, and in some ways is temporary. *Hos* becomes *house*, and as is illustrated in Figure 3–4 *ent* becomes *ant* and then finally *aunt*. *Pesl vay ya* (see Figure 3–3) becomes *pencil vany* (see Figure 3–5) and finally *Pennsylvania* as the child sees that word in print.

Actually, even proficient readers and writers use invented spelling in their writing if the word is one not frequently seen or noticed in print. Some approximate the spelling and let the spell checker make suggestions. (Check your own emails for examples.)

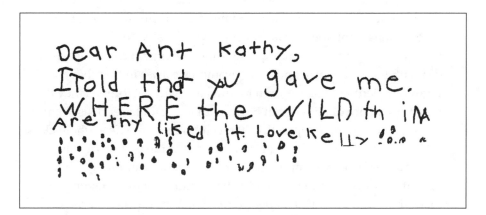

Figure 3–4 Developing spelling of the word *aunt*

Figure 3–5 Developing spelling of the word *Pennsylvania*

Everyday Phonics

The teaching of phonics does not necessarily take preparation. There are many opportunities throughout the day to work on phonics instruction. When there are extra minutes before leaving for a "special," such as art, music, or gym, play games that work with letters and sounds. For example:

1. **I-spy.** Children are usually familiar with this game using color, but it can also be played using letter sounds. If the teacher says, "I spy something that begins with a *p* like *pepper*, the children can make guesses, like *poster*, or *pencil*, or *paper* until they guess the word in mind. In first or second grade this game is still fun for those who know their letter sounds but provides a class activity that is enjoyable for those children who still need the reinforcement. Sometimes simply choosing a letter and thinking of all the words that begin with that letter is a way to pass time waiting for a bus, waiting in line, or traveling in a car, such as we did with the alphabet sound word examples earlier in this chapter.

2. **Drawing pictures.** Ask children to draw as many pictures as they have time for that are of objects that begin with a certain letter. This is an easy activity to provide practice when children complete a whole-class activity at different times and is fun to share at the end of the day.

3. **Alphabet cans.** Label empty juice cans with letters and invite children to write or draw pictures of objects that begin with those letters and place them in a can. Have paper precut to an appropriate size and placed under the cans. This can also be used as a center activity and can be shared at the end of the day.

4. **Going on a vacation.** Begin by saying, "I'm going on a vacation and I'm going to pack my suitcase with something that begins like *animal*." The next in line chooses an *a* word like *apple* and continues the game, "I'm going on a vacation and I'm going to pack my suitcase with something that begins like *bear*." The next child says something that begins with *b*, like, *bathrobe*, and the game continues.

5. **Magnetic letters.** Individual magnetic dry erase boards provide an inexpensive and versatile way for children to practice with words. It's easy to individualize instruction with some children "writing" the alphabet with the letters, others their names and other words, some even simple sentences. Magnetic letters can also be stored on the corner of the chalkboard and children can take turns using them during center time.

6. **Commercially produced toys**. Many handheld toys have sound and provide options for letter recognition, letter–sound correspondence, and spelling practice. Most of these games have several levels of difficulty and can be used by children at different levels of development. Handheld games offer an attractive alternative to encourage struggling readers who are tired of paper-and-pencil practice, and primary-aged children often consider the games cool. The games can be purchased through school funds, placed on PTO wish lists, and some found at garage sales. If possible, try the game before purchasing to check sound quality for clarity and accuracy.

7. **Manipulatives.** Many companies produce alphabet and word tiles that can be stored in boxes. Children can build words based on patterns (rimes) or beginning and ending sounds. Children can arrange sentences using word tiles or choose words with similar patterns, prefixes, suffixes, roots, and so on.

CHAPTER FOUR

Working with Words

Building Reading and Writing Vocabulary

Vocabulary is learned through reading; the more one reads, the more words one learns. However, there *are* ways teachers can *teach* vocabulary. Traditionally, teachers have tried to teach words to children with the use of lists and exercises, but such activities only store the new information in short-term memory (F. Smith 1994). Vocabulary must be useful and taught in contexts that help learners connect and use the new information; they need to construct meaning. Richard Vacca, JoAnn Vacca, and Mary K. Gove (1995) present five principles to guide vocabulary instruction. These five are:

1. "Select words that children will encounter while reading literature and content material" (Vacca, Vacca, and Gove 1995, 235). Readers do not need to know every word they encounter when reading. Preteaching vocabulary, or introducing new words to readers before they read, should be carefully thought out. Many new words are easy to figure out by using context and many long difficult words are not ones that children will meet often and need to construct meaning. Teachers should choose words that are *key words* (words that help define the concept of the story), *useful words* (words they encounter often but may need to pay attention to), *interesting words* (words that create excitement and interest in words), and *vocabulary-building words* (words that give readers a tool to learn more words, and should be fun) (236–37).

2. "Teach words in relation to other words" (237). Children should learn words that are related systematically and belong to categories. They should be able to compare, classify, generalize, and select words.

3. "Teach students to relate words to their background knowledge" (238). Children know a great many things about many topics and new vocabulary must be able to be connected to what they know (schema). We need to find ways to use what children know and build on that as we introduce something new.

4. "Teach words in pre-reading activities to activate knowledge and use them in post-reading discussion, response and retelling" (238). This is different from preteaching words that are provided in a list. These words are carefully chosen to construct meaning and are used in the context of working with the story.

5. "Teach words systematically and in depth" (239). It is not enough to have students write definitions and even write words in sentences. Again, to really learn a new word, learners must connect it to their own experiences or to something in the story, or discuss the word in class, talking about it and its use. Using words as tools for writing also adds these words to the repertoire of words a child can use to express his or her ideas.

6. "Awaken interest and enthusiasm in words" (240). Teachers who are excited about language kindle that excitement in the children they teach. If words are fun and interesting and the teacher models this throughout the day in all interactions with text, children become just as interested in learning new words, in examining how language works, and in experimenting with language.

Structural Analysis—Prefixes, Suffixes, and Root Words

Learning a bit about how words are built can be of great help to a reader. As children read and begin to examine words closely, they discover how words are related and how adding letter groups before (prefix) a base word or root word or letters after it (suffix) change it in predictable ways when the reader understands the meanings of the prefix or the way the suffix affects matters, such as the tense of the word.

Teaching students the meanings of commonly used prefixes can be quite helpful to readers as they encounter new words. It gives them one more strategy to use when decoding an unfamiliar word. However, making children memorize lists of prefixes out of context is not an authentic way of teaching students how language works. Such opportunities present themselves in the context of real reading situations when students can be reminded that there are several cues that can be used to figure out unknown words, structural analysis being one.

Certain root words come from Latin and are used over and over in English. Recognizing some of these Latin roots is interesting and helps students recognize that much of our language makes sense when we understand how language evolves.

Common Latin Roots

Root	Meaning	Example
aqua	water	aquarium
aud	hear	auditorium
dent	tooth	dentist
dict	speak	dictionary
liber	free	liberty
min	small	minimum
mort	death	mortal
multi	many	multiplication
ped	foot	pedal
port	carry	portable
sci	know	science
sign	mark	signature
terr	land	territory
urb	city	suburban
vis	see	vision

Some Common Greek Roots

Root	Meaning	Example
bio	life	biography
graph	write	autograph
geo	earth	geography
meter	measure	thermometer
therm	heat	thermometer

Some Common Prefixes

Prefix	Meaning	Example
ab	away from	absolute, abdomen
anti	against	antibacterial
auto	self	automobile, automatic
*bi	two	bicycle, biannual
com	with, together	community
contra	against	contrast
de	down, undo	descend, deflate
dis	not	disappear, disrespect
extra	outside	extraordinary
im	not	impatient, impolite
in	into, not	inside, insincere
inter	among	intermediate
mega	huge	megaphone, megahits
micro	small	microscope
mis	wrong	mistake
non	not	nonsense, nonprofit
over	above, beyond	overboard

*pre	before	precook, prehistoric	
pro	in favor of	proclaim, proceed	
*re	again	redial, replay	
sub	under	submarine, subtract	
super	above	superintendent, superior	
tele	far	telephone, telescope	
trans	across	transmit, transportation	
*tri	three	triangle, trident	
*un	not	undress, unbutton	
uni	one	unicorn, union	

Some Common Suffixes

Suffix	Meaning	Example	
ant	person who	participant, informant	
arium	place for	aquarium, terrarium	
*ed	in the past	played, walked, dressed	tense marker
er	person who	rider, player, dancer	
er	more than	happier, better	comparative marker (2)
est	most	happiest, cutest	comparative marker (3 or more)
ful	full of	beautiful	
*ing	in the present	singing, writing, sitting	tense marker
less	without	toothless, clueless	
ly	every	daily, weekly, monthly	
*ly	having quality	sadly, quickly, proudly	adverb marker
ness	state of	sadness, happiness	
or	person who	doctor, inventor	
ous	full of	strenuous, courteous	
*s, es	more than one	cats, wishes	plural marker
y	state of	cloudy, windy	

*frequently used; appropriate for primary grades

Word Walls

Word walls are areas of the classroom where words are written or mounted for children to use and work with. Sometimes a bulletin board is used, but often teachers use blank walls in the room that can provide space for word walls to grow and are situated where children can easily see the words. It is important that teachers and children use the wall, not just put up the words. A word wall is a teaching tool and should be used as a part of instruction.

There are many different types of word walls; sometimes the teacher chooses the words, but sometimes the students and teacher choose words together. The words on a word wall are usually written on pieces of cut paper in bold black marker. The words are arranged on the wall alphabetically.

It is important that the teacher remember to:

1. Add a small number of words each week as needed.
2. Put words where students can see them, using colors to differentiate between similar confusing words, such as *were/where, that/this, what/when.*
3. Put up words that children need, especially those needed in their writing.
4. Talk about the words on the wall. Clap the letters together and discuss how the word looks.
5. Work with the words regularly and talk about them as they reappear. Do not simply put words up on the wall and expect that the teaching about that word has been completed.
6. Let students know that when writing, it is expected that word wall words be spelled correctly.

Types of Word Walls

- words commonly confused when reading and writing
- words that are similar (word families)
- high-frequency words
- words from content study (social studies, science) often used in intermediate grades

Kindergarten and First Grade Word Walls   Start the year off using the children's names as the first words on the word wall. Add words weekly that appear frequently in children's reading selections. High-frequency lists may be helpful, but be careful not to just add words at random. Make sure the children recognize them as words they are reading that week and see a purpose to adding them to the wall.

When children ask how to spell words, remind them to look at the word wall. In kindergarten, children often like to use their friends' names in their writing. It is helpful to have word wall words on magnets or magnetic tape, so children can manipulate them. Often they take them to their seats to copy the correct spelling, which is much easier at this age than having to look up and down for each letter.

Second and Third Grade Word Walls Often children's writing rather than reading guides the selection of words on word walls in second and third grade, although both sources are used. Words chosen are those with irregular spellings, particularly those used often in writing. Other words chosen include:

- words representing common blends such as *bl, br, cr, dr, fl, fr, gr, pl, pr, sk, sl, sm, sn, sp, st,* and *tr.*
- contractions as well as homophones such as *too, to, two, their, they're, right, write,* and so on.
- common compound words (*everyone, into, something, sometimes, everything*)

■ words with endings that change in other forms (*silly, sillier, silliest, funny, funnier, funniest*)

Activities with Word Walls

Remember, just posting words on a word wall is not enough to teach vocabulary. Teachers must find ways to work with the words with students, so children can have time and opportunity to make connections and test hypotheses (Cunningham, Hall, and Sigmon 1999). One such teaching strategy is called "on-the-back" word wall activities (125). As words are added to the word wall, there is now time to use these words to extend what children are learning. This particular activity helps children learn to add endings to common words. Choose words from the word wall that are used often in other forms, for instance *brother, drink, jump, rain,* and *eat.*

Have children look at these words as you write them on the board, or if your word wall words can be removed, set these words aside on the board. Explain that these words sometimes need an ending, depending on how we use them in a sentence. For instance:

1. I have two *brothers.* Do you have any *brothers*?
2. I like *drinking* my milk from a straw.
3. After the rain yesterday, I *jumped* over all the puddles in my driveway.
4. It *rained* all day yesterday. Is it *raining* now?
5. I am going to play with my friends after I finish *eating* my lunch.

On a sheet of paper, have children write the word wall word used in each sentence and then write the word using the ending in the sentence. After each sentence, discuss the ending, and write the new form of the word next to the original word. Talk about the endings they needed to use, such as *-s, -ing, -ed.*

Begin this activity using these most common endings, and when appropriate (when words are need in writing) add words that use endings like *-ly, -er,* or *-est.* Use minilessons to talk about words that have irregular endings, such as changing *-y* to *-i,* adding *-est,* or dropping *-e* and doubling consonants. (This is usually done in second or third grade, but it depends on when children are ready and will find the information useful.)

Another on-the-back activity uses word wall words to teach more about rhyming (onset and rimes). Teachers often put stars or asterisks next to words that can be changed to many other words by changing initial consonants. These are called *pattern words.* For instance, the words *cat, make, black, nice,* and *found* may all have stars next to them. After identifying these words as ones we will use that day, the children turn over their papers and the teacher reads a sentence like,

I wore my baseball *hat* to the game. (Emphasize the word *hat* when reading.)

The children discuss the words in the sentence and *hat* in particular. They decide *hat* sounds like *cat* so they write both these words on their paper.

The teacher continues the activity, using sentences the children can relate to such as:

My favorite kind of birthday *cake* is chocolate. (*make*)

I need to *pack* my toothbrush when I go to my friend's house for a sleep-over. (*black*)

I love to eat *rice* with my chicken at dinner. (*nice*)

The *sound* of crickets on a summer night helps me fall asleep. (*found*)

On the front of their papers the children will write the word wall words and on the back, or next to the word, the word that rhymes.

cat	hat
make	cake
black	pack
nice	rice
found	sound

For younger children or those who need more help with the concept of rhyming, the teacher might use one word wall word and several sentences using the same word. For instance, she could use the word *car* and the sentences:

It is hard to open a new *jar* of pickles.

We put a layer of *tar* on our driveway to smooth it out.

In gym, we had to jump over the *bar*.

Is it very *far* to your grandmother's house?

Another on-the-back activity that children enjoy is the word detective activity. This is played like I-spy with the teacher giving clues (see also I-spy in Chapter 3). For instance, the teacher might say, "I spy a word that . . .

. . . we added to our word wall this month.

. . . has four letters.

. . . starts with *th*.

. . . the vowel in the middle is an *e*.

. . . fits in the sentence, Some people are playing baseball today. Are you playing with ___?" (*them*)

Since the teacher gives five clues, the students number one through five on their papers and write a guess after each clue. By the end everyone should know the word, but the children will have to think of all the clues as they progress and eliminate words as they have more information.

Word of the Day

Many teachers have long recognized the power of discussing a new word or revisiting a word each day. Traditionally, the teacher writing the word on the board and the student "looking it up" did this. However, the idea can be much more enjoyable and beneficial if the students are more involved and the word or words are more meaningful.

A part of the morning routine can be the sharing of new words by the teacher *and* the students. Words from reading, TV, other media, and the world around them are interesting because they have a context. For instance, a computer literate fourth grader might share the word (or phrase) *instant messenger* or *IM*. The teacher can add the word *dialoguing* and the class can discuss the meanings, similarities, and differences.

Words are listed and sometimes categorized but the strength of this activity is in the fueling of interest in words. There are no tests or quizzes, no requirements for using the words a certain number of times (this is always an artificial use of language), but children will naturally use the words in speech or writing when they are appropriate. Most important, taking time to notice and analyze words makes vocabulary interesting and develops spoken and written vocabulary of the student.

List–Group–Share (LGS)

The strength of this strategy is that it builds on what children already know. LGS begins with what a student knows about a subject and gives him a chance to organize information. Similar to mapping, LGS categorizes using known and new information. When using this strategy, the teacher or students choose a topic or theme. Then,

- **List.** Students brainstorm all the words they can think of that relate to that topic (this is best done in small groups). Students share their knowledge of words with others in the group who may be unfamiliar with some.
- **Group.** After listing all the words the group can think of, they begin grouping the words into categories. For instance, after listing all the words they can think of for December holidays (Christmas, Hanukkah, Kwaanza), they may see categories such as foods, decorations, songs, dates, traditions, and stories emerge from the list. After grouping, the students can add other words that they now think of with the help of the category. The teacher can point out that once words are organized, the words begin to make sense together and this helps us remember other similar words that belong in that category.
- **Share.** Students can share with other groups and even finds ways to share their lists. They can map the words, chart them, or find some other way to visually display the lists. Here are two examples:

Rainforest

Brainstorm list

trees
tigers
snakes
hot
rain
canopy
jungle
South America
plants

List by categories

PLACES
South America
North America

WEATHER
hot
rain
humid

ANIMALS
tigers
snakes
leopards

VEGETATION
poison plants
plants you can eat (edible)
canopy

Vacation

Brainstorm list

summer
lake
swimming
cottage
skiing
fishing
winter
snowboarding
cabin
family
suitcase
map
Florida

Disneyworld
warm
Williamsburg
souvenirs

List by categories

PLACE

motel
grandparents' house
lake
Disneyworld
cottage
cabin

TIME OF YEAR

summer
winter
spring
warm

ACTIVITIES

swimming
skiing
fishing
snowboarding
boat
hiking

MEANS OF TRAVEL

airplane
car
RV

Visual–Auditory–Kinesthetic–Tactile (VAKT) Approach

Some children have great difficulty recognizing words and seem to be at a loss when it comes to word patterns or seeing smaller words in unfamiliar long words. The VAKT approach uses visual and auditory word recognition strategies that are common, along with kinesthetic (position of body parts, hands, and mouth) and tactile (touch) strategies.

As with most learning, this strategy works best when children's personal choice is respected. Children choose a word they want to learn either from their reading, personal dictionaries, or word wall, and instead of just looking at and saying the word, they also trace and touch the printed word until they can write the word from memory. Sometimes the children trace the word in sand or in shaving cream. As children learn the word they put the word in their word bank.

This approach takes a great deal of time and patience and works best one-on-one with struggling readers. Tracing words with a finger, writing words in the air, and using the sense of touch as well as movement gradually supports children as they learn new words. After much practice children use this strategy on their own when they encounter unknown words.

Word Maps

Older readers, those in grades 4 through 6, still need to develop their reading and writing vocabularies but the traditional method of memorizing lists of words does little to accomplish this. Connecting words to literature, the world, and life experiences helps children to make the necessary connections needed to make the new word theirs. For example, when reading

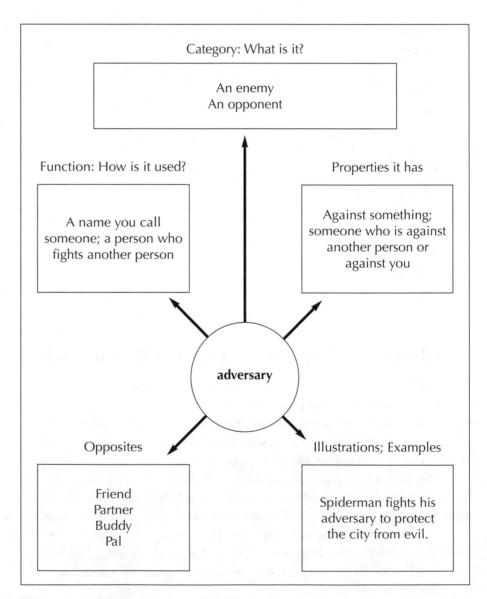

Figure 4–1 Defining a concept: Word map

Shiloh by Phyllis Reynolds Naylor, students will connect with situations in which they have experienced grudges and they know what it feels like to deal with an *adversary*. They may not have experienced a personal *vendetta* but they know through movies when characters are motivated by vendettas. Such words make discussions of the conflicts in a novel like *Shiloh* much more detailed and students remember such vocabulary because they can make connections.

A word map encourages students to understand and remember a word as a concept rather than a simple definition. A word map for the word *adversary* might look like that in Figure 4–1. This technique can be adapted for younger readers with fewer "legs" to map and simpler connections (see Figure 4–2).

Contextual Analysis

When supporting developing or struggling readers, it is important to help them remember that although we pay attention to the way a word looks when we read, we also must pay attention to how it is used in a sentence

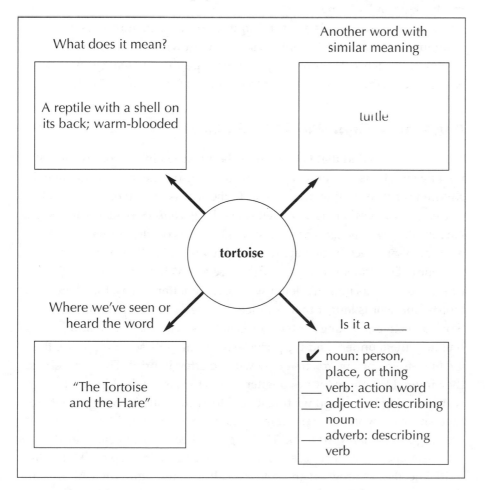

Figure 4–2 Word map for younger readers

or story. Proficient readers always read to make meaning—they make sense of the words. Readers use what they know about the word as they read. For instance, read the following sentence: "I went to the ___ and saw the lions and the ___." Proficient readers will begin to predict what words fit in those blanks by using the context of the sentence and their background knowledge. The possibilities in the first blank are words like *zoo, circus, jungle,* and many animals are possible in the second sentence, but the reader knows from context that the word in the second blank is a noun (syntax) and an animal (semantics). When the reader adds the cues of the first letter of each word, along with the context, the possibilities narrow. For instance, if the sentence read: "I went to the z___ and saw the lions and the t___," the reader would have context and graphic cues of letter–sound patterns to narrow the options. And with background knowledge, the reader would predict that the first word is *zoo*. The second blank has several options, *tiger, turtle,* and *turkey,* but again, with the knowledge the reader has about zoos, the logical choice is *tiger.* Remember, all children do not have the same background knowledge; although *tiger* is obvious to children who have been to a zoo or read about zoos, not every child has this background schema.

Using context clues is a natural strategy for proficient readers, but struggling readers often try only to sound it out without using the clues within the sentence. We must help readers expect text to make sense. Teachers can model this strategy during think-alouds (see Chapter 7).

Bag Words/Sight Word Vocabulary

Teachers understand that vocabulary is best learned in the context of real reading situations, but playing with words is also beneficial. A way to help children practice sight words, similar to the words we put on word walls (see earlier discussion), is an activity called *bag words* (Strickland and Strickland 2000, 151). Teachers can give students words on slips of paper in reclosable sandwich bags that are commonly found in their reading (see Appendix D). Students can play with these words in various ways. They can sort the words into two-letter words, three-letter words, four-letter words, and words longer than four letters. They can look in books and be word detectives, looking for the words in the stories they are reading. This will help them understand the purpose of learning these words, since they are high-frequency words that they will see often in print. The children are then invited to choose four two-letter words to learn by looking at the word, turning it over and writing it, and then checking it. When they feel they know the word, they put it into another bag labeled, "Words I Know," creating a personal word bank. That bag then becomes an instant artifact for self-assessment or teacher assessment. These bags help keep track of individual needs and progress and celebrate all children's growth. Children are delighted to see their bags fill up with words they choose to learn, and they can use these bags to play with one another by way of review.

A word of caution. Like all suggestions, this activity may not be appropriate for all children. For some children, reading words out of context is extremely difficult and the game is not fun when it becomes a chore or is stressful. For these children, look at high-frequency words in the context of real reading and use a checklist to keep track of what a child knows.

Scrambled Sentences

Working at the word level, we can help struggling readers by moving from whole to part to whole. For example, using a familiar text that is mostly memorized or at least read previously so that the meaning is clear, a sentence from the story can be put on a sentence strip, read together, and then cut apart into single words. The child can then practice using the words to rebuild the sentence. This helps children use the three cueing systems as they rebuild the sentences so they make sense (semantic and syntactic cues) and also as they pay attention to the way the word looks (graphic cues).

For example, after reading a sentence written on the strip, such as "I do not like green eggs and ham," the sentence can be cut apart and reconstructed word by word. A child holding the word *green* would have to remember that it modified *eggs*, place it in front of *eggs*, and realize that the green eggs were what was not "liked" and place them after the word *like*.

A version of this exercise can be done with stories that children and their teacher write together. For example, Linda Scott, a teacher we worked with when writing *Making Assessment Elementary* (Strickland and Strickland 2000), wrote a story with her students and then printed the text of the story on the computer in a font large enough so that they could cut apart the words. The students each illustrated the story and pasted the words under their illustrations (see Figure 4–3). As students take their stories home to practice reading, their teacher can communicate with parents through a letter sent home with the story, such as the following letter Linda sent to parents:

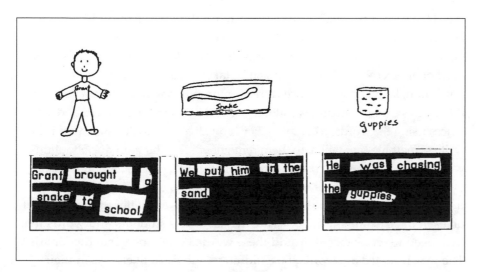

Figure 4–3 An illustrated version of the class story

Dear Parents,

One of our students brought a snake to school for a visit. We wrote a story about it together. Then I typed the story we wrote and printed copies for the class. We cut the words apart and glued them in the correct order. We mixed the pages up and put the story back in order. We even practiced reading the story backwards, to improve word recognition. We looked for patterns in the story. And finally we looked at vowels in the words in the story.

For tonight, please have your child read the story to you. Here are some things to keep in mind:

- Touch each word at the beginning and slide with your finger as your child reads the words.
- Match the word your child is reading with your finger as you point to it.
- Help your child recognize that the pictures match what the words are saying.
- Have your child use a crayon or highlighter to find the beginning sounds.

In addition, your child should be able to touch some of the words out of order, and recognize them.

Please remember that reading this book at home should be a stress-free, fun activity that also has expectations! Talk with your child about what we did in school. Mention some of the things I listed. Discuss as much as possible. Let me know how it goes. Write comments on the back and have your child return the stories tomorrow.

Thanks,

Mrs. Scott

Word Banks and Personal Dictionaries

Word banks and personal dictionaries can help build a child's sight vocabulary and increase the child's ability to see word patterns. Students can create personal word banks by writing words they have learned and think they will need on index cards. These words can be taken from trade books, basal stories, nonfiction, language experience stories, environmental print, or any text that the child is using. Sometimes children write definitions of the word and sentences using the words in context. They may also want to illustrate words or write something that will help them remember something unique about this word. The cards can then be put into a file box and kept in students' desks.

For younger students, a personal dictionary is more manageable. Students can be given notebooks in which they write one letter of the alphabet on each page (commercial books are available). As students find words that they need to remember, they add these words to their personal dictionaries. The words added are words the children would most likely use in their writing, and their personal dictionary becomes a writing tool.

Word Sorts

Word sorts promote word recognition and help develop vocabulary through awareness of word patterns and similarities. Word sorts are activities that give children an opportunity to play with words as they categorize them. It should be nonthreatening and presented as a challenge or game rather than as a required exercise. It is an activity that is done in pairs or groups and can help children learn from each other. The categories for word sorts can be set up by the teacher or by the students themselves. Students can also create their own categories for word sorts and ask other students to guess what the category is by looking at the group of words. The words used in the sorts can be vocabulary from word banks, novels, spelling words, and so on. Examples of categories include words that:

- have a prefix/suffix
- have other words in them
- have the same beginning sound
- have one syllable in one pile, two syllables in a second pile, three syllables in a third pile
- have a short vowel sound, words with long vowel sound, words with both short and long vowel in the same word
- can be sorted by parts of speech: nouns, verbs, adjectives, adverbs
- have more than one meaning; more than one pronunciation
- contain smaller words

Sometimes students can sort words and other groups have to guess the category. Word sorts help students get repeated exposure to words as well as give them an opportunity to look at words closely from a certain perspective. Looking at words in a variety of ways helps students to analyze words and think about them. This is especially important for struggling readers who don't do this automatically and need opportunities to think about words.

There are two kinds of sorts—open and closed. The purpose in both of these activities is discovery. The steps for *open sorts* are:

1. Children take their bag words or word banks to a place on the floor.
2. Children group their words in different ways (let them come up with ways to sort).
3. After grouping words, one child volunteers to read his group of words and others in the class guess the criteria for the grouping.
4. There is no one correct way to do open sorts; children come up with a variety of ways to sort—word length, syllables, beginning letter, endings, nouns, action words, and so on. Older students have more fun as they come up with unique categories for sorts.

In *closed sorts*, all students look for words according to a category given to them by the teacher.

The process of simply sorting and physically arranging the words is good for many children who work best with active learning. The purpose of sorts is not to teach phonics rules, but to give students a chance to discover graphic similarities.

Making Words

Making words includes a number of activities that are fun for students and help their word recognition, spelling, and vocabulary development (Cunningham and Cunningham 1992).

Secret Words

In this activity, students make words using a given number of letters, and then they manipulate these words to make new words. Both little words and big words are made, but the goal of the activity is to find the word that uses all the letters, the secret word (Cunningham and Hall 1998). Remember, the teacher should:

1. Decide on a secret word that uses all the letters and builds on students' interests, background, and letter–sound patterns.
2. Brainstorm all the words that can be made from those letters before giving children the letters.
3. Choose twelve to fifteen words that have
   a. a pattern
   b. both little and big words to differentiate instruction
   c. words that use the same letters but in different order
   d. some proper nouns to emphasize capitalization
4. Write the chosen words on index cards and order them from the shortest to the longest.
5. Order words with same rime pattern, so children will recognize that changing the onset results in a new word.
6. Choose some letters or patterns for sorts.
7. Include three or four more difficult words a child could read or spell based on the rhyming word (transfer words).
8. Store cards in an envelope and write the words in order, the patterns included.

Examples
Secret word: *sandwich*
Letters: *c, d, s, i, h, n, a, w*
Make:

an	dish	cash
in	sand	dash
is	Dan	wash
his	can	aid
hid	hand	din
saw	wand	sin

Chad	acid	chin
disc	wish	win

Sort for rhyming words:

can	cash	din
Dan	dash	sin
hand	chin	
sand	win	

Related words: *chin, chins, win, wins, hand, hands, wand, wands*
Transfer words: *candle, Canada, window, withstand, dandelion*

Secret word: *children*
Letters: *n, r, l, i, c, d, h, e*
Make:

chide	din	die
ride	lid	dine
hide	rid	dice
lend	hid	rice
rend	child	nice
hen	Chile	cinder
end	chin	hinder
den	lend	

Sort for rhyming words:

end	lid	ride
lend	rid	chide
hen	hid	
den	hide	

Related words: *hid, hide, child, children*
Transfer words: *advice, comprehend, defend, Sweden, inside*

Reading in Square Blocks

This activity builds on the fact that some children find that manipulating a limited number of letters helps them focus on important characteristics in words. The teacher selects a word that is five to eight letters long and is taken from a selection the child has read previously (this puts the word into a meaningful context and gives a reason for concentrating on it). The teacher passes out one-inch squares of paper for each letter to each group and calls out the letters one at a time and the students write the letters on a square of paper. They now have five to eight letters to work with. They can begin with making two-letter words with the letters and work their way up to three-letter, four-letter, five-letter, and six-letter words.

When manipulating letters this way, the teacher has the opportunity to teach minilessons about word families, prefixes, syllables, and so on. Teachers can also use transparencies cut into squares and the teacher and student, working with an overhead projector, can manipulate the letters together. Pocket charts work much the same way. Individual or pairs of students can use letter squares from Scrabble or reading manipulatives produced by many manufacturers that include individual letter blocks. A recorder should write the words down so the squares can be reused.

For example, if the word *reading* was given as r-e-a-d-i-n-g to be written in square blocks, students might come up with the following:

Two-Letter Words

in
an

Three-Letter Words

red
ear
rid
age
aid
gin
dig
rig
air

Four-Letter Words

read
grin
rind
dare
aide
ding
dear
near
gear
ring

Five-Letter Words

grade
grind
grain
drain

Adapted Commercially Produced Word Games

Although there are many good word games that may be purchased, many variations of commercially produced games can be made by the teacher and the students. The following are some examples.

Word Bingo

This game is based on the familiar Bingo game board with five squares across and five down. The teacher selects words from a story to be read to the class, so there are five categories with five words in each category. Names of characters might be an obvious category as might be colors mentioned in the story. More creative categories might be Ways Authors Say a Character Is Speaking—*said, asked, yelled, stated, replied*. The teacher reads each word in the category and the students decide which block to write them in, so long as they are in the proper category. One child might put *said* in the first block, another in the fourth block. Once each student has his or her card filled with the twenty-five words, the teacher rereads the story, stopping to highlight a game word. When the student hears the word, he covers the word on his board with a coin or marker. As the children get five across, down, or diagonal, they shout out, "Bingo!" The game continues until everyone has a bingo.

Scrabble or Scrabble Jr.

Board games such as Scrabble or Scrabble Jr. have been around for years, and the junior version is even more appropriate for elementary students. The game can be played as originally designed or the letter tiles can be used for other purposes, as suggested in the previous section.

Stick Person

Based on another traditional favorite, hangman, stick person can be played with two or more players who are required to guess an unknown word by calling out possible letters. The person who is the challenger writes blanks for the letters in the word. If a letter is called out that is in the word, the letter is put in the appropriate space(s). If the letter is not part of the word, a body part is put on the stick figure. If the stick person is completed (body, head, arms, legs) before the word is guessed, the challenger is awarded another turn. If someone guesses correctly, that person gets to choose the next word for the challenge and the new stick figure. More body parts—eyes, hands, and feet—can be added for younger players; harder words can be chosen for older players. (See Figure 4–4.)

Phrase of Fortune

This version of the popular game Wheel of Fortune doesn't use a wheel for prizes. Instead, the teacher or the person who is the challenger writes a phrase using blanks for each letter on the board or a transparency. Three individuals or teams take turns guessing a consonant (no vowels are

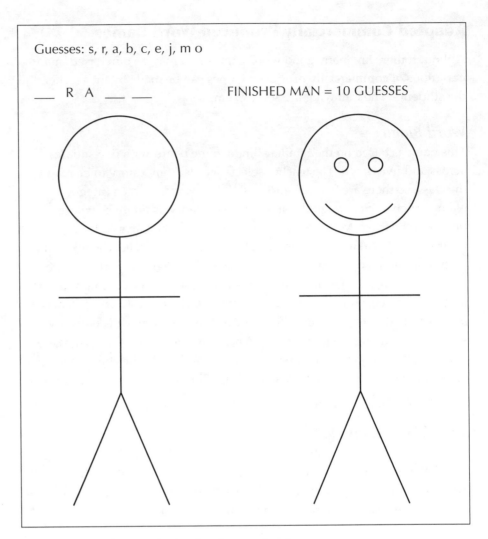

Figure 4–4 Stick man playing for the word *train*

guessed; they must be filled in by looking at the consonant position and making sense of the phrase). As soon as an individual or a team guesses a correct letter and thinks the phrase is known, they may guess, but are out of the game if they guess incorrectly. As in the stick person game, the winner gets to be the new challenger who constructs the next phrase.

> For example: P_ _N_T B_TT_ _ _N_ J_LL_ S _N_ W_ _ _
> (Guesses include the letters that did not appear: *g, f, k, m, v*)
> ANSWER: peanut butter and jelly sandwich

Vocabulary Feud

This version of the popular game Family Feud needs some preparation to play in class. The teacher creates or obtains a list of sentence completion exercises from a textbook series appropriate for the grade level. With the help of a cooperating teacher, students in an upper grade complete the sentences and the various answers supplied are tabulated, assigning point values to the number of responses. The original game records the top three to six answers given by one hundred respondents, but such formality is not necessary. With the results in hand, the teacher challenges two teams of students to complete the missing word in each sentence from the sentence completion exercises, saying that she knows the top three (or however many) answers. The first team to correctly identify a word controls the play and each member of the team takes turns guessing words that complete the sentence. If the team correctly identifies all the possible responses given, they win the points associated with each response. However, if the team misses three times, the opposing team gets a chance to steal the points by correctly identifying one more response. The answers can be prepared on a transparency to be revealed or written as guessed on an overhead or chalkboard, with the associated points or number of responses given by the upper-grade students. The winning team gets to challenge the next group of students from the class. Teams may be shifted and rearranged so that no one group dominates.

Six Degrees of Words

Another type of word game functions like the six degrees of separation game in which every person is connected to every other person by six turns of "I know someone who knows someone." It is easier to show than to explain. Every word can theoretically be changed into another word that contains the same number of letters, mutating one letter at a time. For example, *dog* can become *cat* by this sequence: *dog—dot—cot—cat.* And there are numerous variations: *dog—dug—bug—hug—hut—hat—cat.* Children can play this with each other individually or as teams, challenging each other by saying something like, "I can change a *cow* into a *pig*; can you?" Here's how it is done: *cow—sow—bow—bog—big—wig—pig*

Human Words

Another type of word game that extends children's vocabulary is *human words*, developed by Jennifer Walsh (Sipe 2003). After teaching a vocabulary/spelling-related rule, Jennifer gives each student in the class a letter card—a sheet of colored construction paper featuring a brightly written individual letter. Jennifer chooses a word for the class, and the students who hold one of the letters in the word come to the front of the classroom and arrange themselves in the proper word order to spell the word correctly. For example, if she were to choose the word *ride*, the students with one of those letters would come to the front of the room to spell r-i-d-e. She could then teach the suffix *-ing* by asking the class to change the word to *riding* and the children, especially the one holding the silent *e*, would need to decide whether to stay or to go when the suffix is added. The teacher could also teach onsets by asking the children to change *ride* to *hide* to *side*. Prefixes could be added with *out-* or *in-* to *side* to form *outside* or *inside*. Jennifer believes, "Active participation is the important factor in 'human words.' This activity encourages thinking about words, reflecting on the use of a rule or pattern, and making decisions about applications of a rule or pattern; and, . . . the movement creates an interesting way to promote reflection and learning" (Sipe 2003, 69).

Context-Structure-Sound-Reference (CSSR)

The context-structure-sound-reference (CSSR) technique (Ruddell 1993) was first suggested by William Gray (1946) as a process to help children answer the question, "What do you do when you come to a word you don't know?"

When I come to a word I don't know, I check:

Context
I read to the end of the sentence and
■ check for meaning clues in the sentence
■ check for meaning clues in the previous sentences
■ use clues to find what I think the word means.

If it makes sense, I keep reading. If not, I go to:

Structure
I look at parts of the word for meaning clues such as
■ prefixes, root words
■ suffixes, an ending that might help
■ I put these clues together with context clues.

If it makes sense, I keep reading. If not, I go to:

Sound
I try to say the word and listen for meaning clues
■ I hear the word as I try to pronounce it
■ I ask if it is a word I know the meaning of
■ I put these clues together with context and structure clues.

If it makes sense, I keep reading. If not, I go to:

Reference
I go to other places to find a reference to the word such as
■ notes at the bottom or in the margin
■ a glossary of words in the back of the book
■ the dictionary
■ asking someone the meaning of the word.

In any event, I keep reading.

Figure 4–5 The CSSR chart

We know that proficient readers begin by using information *in* the text to figure out unknown words; they use *context*. After using clues in the text, proficient readers look at the *structure* of the word, and try the *sound* of the word, using graphic cues for the pronunciation. If that doesn't help, they either keep reading, ask someone, or check a *reference* book if the word is absolutely necessary for the meaning.

Sometimes a chart in the room reminding developing readers of these strategies is helpful (see Figure 4–5). Use it as a teaching strategy but also encourage children to use it when reading independently or with a buddy.

Word Study After Reading

Most basal reading series encourage the preteaching of vocabulary that is new by introducing these words in isolation on flipcharts. It is true that often words must be introduced before reading, but teachers should determine which vocabulary is essential for understanding that could not be figured out by seeing the word in context and using the three cueing systems (which, after all, is how we want children to understand that readers continue to learn words all the time). Frequently used words that link our language, such as *that, which,* or *with,* do not benefit from preteaching and should be introduced in context of the story. Often readers will figure them out because of the flow of a sentence, but that is not to say that discussion of such words after reading would not be helpful, perhaps looking more closely at the word, discussing beginning sounds and homonyms such as *which* and *witch.*

If a word such as *Antarctic,* or *amphibian,* or *apprehensive* were to be used in the context of a story but not defined within the context, it would be helpful to preteach such a word, especially if it was essential to understanding. Often words are best taught or discussed after reading as part of word study that is, at that point, in context. Such decisions are best made by teachers who know the readers in the group and are aware of what they need and by teachers who have previewed the story and determined what words cannot be figured out in context.

CHAPTER FIVE

Fluency

Although teachers will agree that one of the major problems of struggling readers is fluency, few reading programs deal directly with strategies that will help with this problem. One of the reasons for this is that often halting, choppy reading is the outward symptom of a reading problem rather than the problem itself. Often children who read word by word ignore punctuation, or falter over many words and are not reading for meaning, so that their very approach to the act of reading affects their fluency. In many cases, fluency improves as children use skills, such as prediction, and begin to read as if they expected meaning.

This is not to say that, at the same time teachers are working on comprehension strategies or meaning making (covered in Chapters 6 through 8), they cannot be giving children an opportunity to hear themselves as smooth fluent readers, one of the ingredients necessary for seeing oneself as a good reader. This section of strategies suggests ways teachers can assist students in reading smoothly while they grow in confidence as proficient meaning-making readers.

Assessing Fluency

Teachers know if students need help with fluency by listening to the child read aloud, but often teachers are asked to provide a quantitative measure of fluency improvement. I would recommend not using a stopwatch to time readers. It is unnerving, distracting, and gives the wrong message to young readers. They begin to see reading as a race or that speed is a primary concern. As I stated earlier, fluency should improve with practice as a result of meaning making. However if rates are required, tape-record the reader and figure out the rate to report later. The rate can be determined using the following formula (Rasinski and Padak 2000, 105): (total words read in the passage x 60) ÷ total time to read measured in seconds = rate in words per minute. For example: If there were seventy-four words in passage, which were read in two minutes ten seconds, the calculation would be: (74 x 60) ÷ 130 = 34.1 words per minute.

As a measure for comparison, Timothy Rasinski and Nancy Padak (2000) provide oral reading rates, following second-semester grade level estimates:

Grade 1: 80 words per minute
Grade 2: 90 words per minute
Grade 3: 110 words per minute
Grade 4: 140 words per minute
Grade 5: 160 words per minute
Grade 6: 180 words per minute

This words-per-minute formula is useful when it is necessary to report fluency levels, but teachers can also assess fluency through observation, including aspects such as punctuation and expression and these results can be shared with the reader during reading conferences.

Modeling Fluent Reading by Reading Aloud

Many struggling readers don't know how fluent reading sounds. They may not have been read aloud to since they were quite young (or even at all) and often are grouped with other children who are struggling readers themselves who do not read fluently. Research has also agreed that reading aloud to children helps them appreciate literature, develop their own language, and build understandings about reading and writing (Cramer 1975; Hancock 2000; Copenhaver 2001).

All children enjoy hearing a good story and hearing fluent reading is essential at certain stages of reading development. Teachers or other proficient guest readers can read with expression, enthusiasm, and pull the listener into the story—the effect of fluent reading. In some cases, it is appropriate for children to hear a text aloud before they read it independently, especially in primary grades. This prereading helps children anticipate, and knowing the story line helps them to read for meaning.

Reading aloud doesn't need to end at second or third grade. Older readers love to hear a good book read aloud. In fact, many proficient adult readers look back fondly on those times their fifth- or sixth-grade teacher read a chapter or two of a wonderful novel aloud after lunch to the class. Proficient readers, as well as struggling readers, can enjoy the experience of a good story read aloud and fluently and the struggling readers will get a taste of what fluent reading can do for a story.

Computer and Tape-Recorded Readings

Tape-recorded readings can be another way to model fluent reading. Although commercially prepared audiotapes are readily available for many trade books, books read aloud on tape by the teacher have many advantages (including cost). Commercial tapes often have sounds other than those of the readers, which can prove distracting for the listener, and the teacher can make sure the story is read at an appropriate natural speed.

Computer readings can also be used to model fluent reading. Although many computer texts are excellent, teachers should preview these. Some include deviations from or additions to the original text that could prove confusing for the reader, and others are read at a pace that is choppy and unnatural—exactly the wrong model for the struggling reader.

Writing Text for Struggling Readers

It is widely accepted that it is best to let struggling readers read text that interests them, but when children are reading at a primer level, the books or stories that are appropriate for their reading levels are usually not very interesting. We know that fluency is aided by repeated reading, but kids are not going to reread a book that is boring or uninteresting.

Developing readers love to read about themselves and will often read text about their lives over and over. For example, the following simple paragraph could be written on the computer and printed in a large font. It could then become Brooke's reading text for several days:

> Brooke is seven years old. She lives on Evergreen Court and is in second grade. Her best friend is Haley. Brooke loves to ride her bike and play with her cat named Gracie.

She could illustrate this simple paragraph, cut the paragraph apart into sentences, and rebuild the paragraph or even cut the sentence apart and rebuild using individual words. When Brooke can read this paragraph fluently, her next text can continue "her story":

> When Brooke and her brother Ryan play with Gracie they all run around the house. Brooke really likes to have Gracie sleep with her at night, but sometimes the cat meows in her ear very early in the morning.

This procedure can continue until Brooke has a book that is several pages long, all about her, and one that she can read frequently. Brooke can add some of the words to her word bank and continue reading about her interests and adventures.

Teachers tell me that young boys often are uninterested in many of the stories that are published for struggling readers. Writing about riding a four-wheeler, camping in the woods, raising pigeons on the roof, or participating in other activities that are a part of a particular young boy's world will make interesting topics for reading.

Repeated Readings

Teachers have long since recognized that having children do repeated readings until the text can be read smoothly and with expression is one of the best ways for children to improve fluency. Very young children will do this quite naturally, loving to read a favorite book, like Bill Martin Jr.'s *Brown Bear, Brown Bear*, over and over. The more they read it, the smoother their reading becomes and the more comfortable and confident they are. With older children, this text can be a poem, a section of a book, a magazine, or a newspaper. The following steps have been suggested for repeated readings (Samuels 1979):

1. Students choose a short selection (fifty to two hundred words) from stories that are on an appropriate instructional level (not too easy).
2. Students read the passage several times silently until they are comfortable reading it orally.
3. Students may compare tape recordings of their first oral readings with ones read after practice to hear for themselves the difference in fluency.

Younger children usually enjoy reading catchy text over and over, but as children get older, it is much more difficult to make repeated readings meaningful. To older children, the practice appears as a waste of time, repeating a task that has already been accomplished, no matter how poorly. "I've already read this, why should I read it again?" they often ask. It is up to teachers to provide a meaningful context for repeated reading. Samuels (1979) suggests teachers explain this practice by comparing it to the method athletes use to develop their skills, spending time practicing the basics of the sport until they develop speed and smoothness. Letting older children hear the fruits of the labor, by way of justifying such efforts, makes repeated reading a more authentic practice for older children. Two strategies to help develop oral reading fluency in an authentic, nonthreatening way are readers' theatre and choral reading.

Readers' Theatre

Readers' theatre is similar to a radio show. Performers must read their script with enthusiasm and expression. They also must follow along in the script waiting for their lines. Children must read the script over and over, not to memorize it, but to read it smoothly and with expression. There are many ways to prepare for readers' theatre; scripts of popular tales can be found on the Internet at *www.readinglady.com/Readers_Theater/Scripts /scripts.html* and *www.literacyconnections.com/ReadersTheater.html* or books of stories are produced commercially. Teachers can also rewrite favorite stories (*The Little Red Hen, Miss Nelson Is Missing*) or use stories from the basal reader; any story will work if it has good dialogue and perhaps a narrator to fill in parts of the story for the audience. It is best to use scripts with eight or fewer parts and divide the class into groups to perform different scripts so they can share them with each other. Teachers can assign parts or children can volunteer, whatever works best to meet the teacher's objectives. Even the shyest reader, who has only a line or two, still needs to read the entire script as he follows along waiting for his part.

Unlike a play, few or no props are used with readers' theatre. Sometimes a simple name tag or other identifying piece can be used to distinguish the characters from one another. For instance, you can use wolf ears on a headband for the big bad wolf, a red sweater around the shoulders of Little Red Riding Hood, and a sign hung around the neck of the woodcutter simply saying "woodcutter." Children can decide for themselves how the audience will identify each character.

Scripts are always used for readers' theatre, since the objective is reading, so students should not be encouraged to memorize. Older children can participate in writing scripts and eventually choose stories that they would like to rewrite in script form and perform for the class or other classes. The most important thing to remember is that this activity should be risk-free and provide an opportunity for all children to feel that they are accomplished readers.

This is just a portion of dialogue from *The Gingerbread Boy Play* that was submitted by Deb Smith (2004) to be shared with classrooms through the ReadingLady website:

> **Little Old Man:** I love gingerbread. Yum! Yum!
> (The microwave beeps.)
> **Little Old Woman:** Oh, the Little Gingerbread Boy is done.
> **Narrator 1:** Out jumped the Little Gingerbread Boy.
> **Narrator 2:** Out of the door and down the street he ran.

Some of the other scripts that were available on the Internet in early 2004 were works such as *3 Little Javelinas*, *3 Pigs*, *Arthur's Christmas* by Marc Brown, *Cinderella BigFoot*, *Cows That Type*, *Dog Breath*, *Frog & Toad*, *Goldilocks & The 3 Bears*, *The Great Kapok Tree*, *Gullible's Troubles*, *The Hat*, *Humpty Dumpty*, Jack Prelutsky poems, *ListenBuddy*, *Mayzie*, *Owen*, *Redheaded Robbie's Christmas Story*, *Stellaluna*, *The Frog Prince Continued*, *The Red Hen Ball*, *Three Billy Goats*, *True Story of the 3 Pigs*, and *Wendell*. There is no need to re-create these works; simply browse the Internet to see what is currently available free for educational use. Practicing these scripts will provide readers with repeated practice, which will boost fluency, interest, and reading confidence.

Choral Reading

Another strategy to help develop oral reading fluency and build confidence is choral reading. Many stories lend themselves to choral reading in which readers read aloud in unison. Such texts have strong rhythm and/or rhyme and often have repeated stanzas. Choral reading can support students with words that are unfamiliar to them in their reading vocabulary. For younger children, many big books have stories that can be read chorally, such as

Chicken Soup with Rice by Maurice Sendak, and *Is Your Mama a Llama?* by Deborah Guarino. Other possibilities are nursery rhymes (printed out on a flipchart or on sentence strips in a pocket chart), jump rope chants, or songs with refrains. Choral reading is also popular with older children in the form of poetry, such as *A Light in the Attic* by Shel Silverstein or *Make a Joyful Noise: A Poem in Two Voices* by Paul Fleischman.

Music, movement, and sound effects, such as clapping, can also accompany choral reading. Such readings can also be dramatized or used with a felt board, such as *I Know an Old Lady Who Swallowed a Fly* by Nadine Wescott. A few suggested books that can be chorally read include:

Brown Bear, Brown Bear, Bill Martin Jr.

Goodnight Moon, Margaret Wise Brown

Hattie and the Fox, Mem Fox

Hush Little Baby (alternate version), Margot Zemach

I Went Walking, Sue Williams

If You Give a Mouse a Cookie, Laura Joffe Numeroff

Jake Baked a Cake, B. G. Hennessy

Mary Wore Her Red Dress, Merle Peek

Mrs. Wishy-Washy, Joy Cowley

Over the Meadow, Ezra Jack Keats

Polar Bear, Polar Bear, Bill Martin Jr.

Rosie's Walk, Pat Hutchins

Seven Little Rabbits, John Becker

Sheep in a Jeep, Nancy Shaw

The Doorbell Rang, Pat Hutchins

The Fat Cat, Jack Kent

The Grouchy Ladybug, Eric Carle

The Jigaree, Joy Cowley

The Little Red Hen, Paul Galdone

The Very Hungry Caterpillar, Eric Carle

The Wheels on the Bus, Maryann Kovakski

This Old Man, Pam Adams

Thump, Thump, Rat-a-tat-tat, Gene Baer

Who Is Coming? Patricia McKissack

Whose Mouse Are You? Robert Kraus

Poetry is also enjoyable and appropriate for choral reading. A wonderful resource, with reproducible poetry, is Gay Su Pinnell and Irene Fountas' (2004) series *Sing a Song of Poetry*, available in three levels—kindergarten, first grade, and second grade.

Paired Reading: Adult and Child

Adults and children reading together not only provides an enjoyable reading experience but it moves the reading experience into what Lev Vygotsky (1978) describes as the child's "zone of proximal development." Simply put, this means that what children can do along with adults today, they can do independently tomorrow. Young readers look to adult models to help them grow as readers, but often adults are not sure how to help. Many parents, adult volunteers in classrooms, and high school helpers resort to the quizzing techniques they remember and mistakenly think were helpful to them as children. In reality, this type of "help" can raise reading anxiety and turn kids off to reading.

As teachers, we need to give adults specific instructions for reading with developing readers. This reading experience should help children learn reading strategies, while providing an enjoyable and authentic reading experience. The instructions in Figure 5–1 provide adults with a framework for paired/shared reading.

Tracking

Reading involves being able to visually follow along the line of text; unfortunately, some children have difficulty with reading that can be attributed to problems with tracking that cause them to lose their place or get confused. Although there is no magic way to teach tracking, the best way is to sweep one's finger along the line of text while reading to the child, beginning in infancy and, as the child grows, involving the child as a reader, talking about the words, and encouraging the child to begin tracking with his or her finger.

If children are of school age, but have little experience with reading, we can start, as we would with younger children, by first reading to them and modeling by sweeping our index finger as we read left to right, from the top of the page to the bottom. Teachers can't take for granted that children will enter school with these reading experiences and employing assessments such as a concepts of print/bookhandling survey (Y. Goodman 1992) will help determine where to begin.

Teachers can help children practice tracking by asking a volunteer to use a pointer while reading together with a group during morning message, an interactive writing lesson, or a shared reading using a Big Book. Such an experience not only benefits the volunteer pointer but also reinforces tracking for all the readers in the group.

When children have difficulty with tracking, losing their place or getting confused, technological aids can support them as they practice reading. Many computer versions of popular books highlight the text as it is being read, helping the reader follow along. Educational computer games, such as Leap Pad, have the child use a pencil-type pointer to designate the word being selected for the computer to read.

A simple, efficient, inexpensive tool to help a child track, especially when reading silently, is the bookmark. Placed under a line of text, this helps readers focus on a particular group of words. This simple method of moving the bookmark over and down as they read assists older children who lose their place easily and provides a sense of security as they develop tracking skills.

1. Begin with a book of the child's choice. This can be a book chosen among three or four titles that the adult suggests and briefly introduces. If the choice is not the child's, but a required reading, the adult must try to stimulate interest by talking, perhaps, about the title, author, and cover illustrations. Try to make personal connections immediately—"Do you like to go to the movies?" (*If You Take a Mouse to the Movies* by Laura Numeroff) or "What movies have you seen?"

2. Take a picture walk through the text. Look through the text at the pictures and talk about the illustrations. What does the book seem to be about? Characters? Events? What looks funny? Interesting?

3. Begin by reading aloud to the child; read every word, sweeping your finger under the text as you read. When appropriate, stop and let the child fill in a word that would make sense so the child is learning to read for meaning. Depending on the development of the child, let him/her point to the words as you are reading together. (Avoid a choppy reading, but read slowly enough for the child to think and process.)

4. As the reading progresses, and if the child is developmentally able, let the child read a page or paragraph and then you do the same. As the child is reading, be patient. Do not tell the child a word the second she hesitates. Give the child time, but don't wait so long that the flow of the story is interrupted. After a few seconds, tell the child the word. This is not the time to quiz the child about phonics or strategies. Read for enjoyment—do not interrogate. Go back and read the sentence again to review at the end of the paragraph.

5. Make the reading experience interactive. Stop and discuss what is going on in the story. The key here is discussion—once again, do not quiz the child! Talk about the book as two readers, not as a teacher and a student. Make predictions about what each of you think might happen next.

6. At the completion of the book or story, do what any two readers would do—talk about it. What did you think? Were our predictions correct? What would you do if you were that character? Don't just question, share your ideas as well.

7. If appropriate, reread the story. Rereading is a helpful practice for building fluency, but is more acceptable with young readers than with intermediate readers. With older readers, you may want to return to important sections and reread them for the sake of discussion.

Figure 5–1 A framework for paired/shared reading

Silent Reading

As children get older and are able to read silently, there may be a marked difference between their oral reading rate and their silent reading rate. Oral reading, for older readers, is often more about performance than about meaning making (even for proficient readers). Struggling readers are often self-conscious and cannot use strategies they have been taught, like skipping a word or reading ahead when doing an oral reading. Try to determine if there is a marked difference between oral and silent reading rates and encourage more silent reading with older struggling readers if you feel fluency is aided and comprehension is better. If a struggling reader must read aloud, provide time for prereading the selection silently first, so the child doesn't have to perform a cold reading in front of a group.

CHAPTER SIX

Before Reading

Procedures to Support Comprehension

Comprehension is an end product of meaning making. As teachers, we cannot teach comprehension; readers themselves bring meaning to the text they read. What we can do is teach readers strategies that help the active process of comprehending, which results in comprehension (K. Goodman 1994).

In this chapter and those that follow, I outline some basic procedures for supporting reading comprehension at different stages—before reading (prereading), during reading, and after reading (postreading)—that provide a framework for instruction. Following those basic procedures are ideas for activities to facilitate comprehension.

Strategies to Use Before Reading

Teachers can model strategies to help young readers develop habits that support their understanding of what they are about to read. Proficient readers regularly do things before reading that developing readers do not; for instance, if I'm in a bookstore looking at a book, I preview it by looking at the cover, the index, if it has one, the description on the back of the book, and so on. Using these strategies, I get an idea of what the book is about and I begin making predictions about meaning. Less experienced readers often simply pick up a book, turn to the first sentence of the first paragraph on the first page, and start reading, trying to activate the process of meaning making without the aid of previewing. This is where teachers must begin to teach students to read strategically.

Young readers can get ready to read by learning procedures such as surveying and predicting, activating prior knowledge, and setting a purpose for reading. The checklist at the end of Chapter 8 (see Figure 8–15) helps students monitor their learning by thinking about the strategies that they are using (or not using).

Surveying and Predicting

Teachers can demonstrate to children that readers have ways to figure out what books are about before they begin reading. They can explain that the cover of the book offers clues and then invite the children to turn to a partner and spend a few moments sharing ways that the cover can help a reader. When students share ideas, they should include the book's title, cover illustration, even the author's name in their discussion and think about how these things help readers get an idea of what the story will be about. Students sometimes recognize that pictures on the cover help with setting, characters, and events. The title tells us what the story will probably be about and knowing what authors write about sometimes helps us (for example, Eric Carle's books are about insects). Younger children can do a *picture walk*, looking at the illustrations and making predictions about the story. Older students can look through the text at illustrations, chapter titles, the back of the book, sections that are bold-faced, charts, graphs, and so on.

Activating Prior Knowledge

Activating prior knowledge is sometimes harder for younger readers because their background knowledge is less complex than that of adults. Teachers need to help children understand that sometimes they can think of what they already know about a subject before reading and that will help them with new ideas presented in the text. For instance, when looking at *The Very Busy Spider* by Eric Carle, they can think about what they already know about spiders (they build sticky webs, they crawl, they live inside and outside) and then get ready to add to what they already know (see KWL charts discussed in the next section). In some cases, activating prior knowledge may not be as concrete and clear. For example, when students look at the title and cover of a work of fiction like *Something from Nothing* by Phoebe Gilman they may not have prior knowledge about the setting, but they do have knowledge about older people ("Who might this be on the cover?") and the relationships that older people have with children. It might be necessary for the teacher to build knowledge (schema) before asking the children to read this story, but the story itself will add to their understanding of the world.

Setting a Purpose for Reading

Teachers can help children understand that we read to confirm or adjust our predictions. When we previewed and activated prior knowledge we took what we knew and added possibilities to it; now, when reading, we begin there and think about what we will be reading for. For instance, in *Something from Nothing*, the reader will be reading to discover what the title means, trying to resolve how we can possibly get something from nothing and how the old man on the cover accomplishes this. (The teacher may have already explained the setting.)

KWL

A strategy that activates prior knowledge and then builds on that prior knowledge is the KWL chart (see Figure 6–1). KWL provides a reason for reading by helping the reader read to confirm or adjust predictions.

KWL stands for What We **K**now, What We **W**ant to Find Out, What We Have **L**earned. (Sometimes we add H for **H**ow we will learn what we wish to find out, and then the activity would technically become KWHL, although most still refer to it as KWL.)

A teacher begins by introducing a topic; an example might be World War II as a topic before reading *Number the Stars* by Lois Lowry. The teacher could give a brief introduction, mentioning perhaps the appropriate dates and the fact that some of the students' great-grandparents or grandparents may have lived during this time. The teacher might continue by explaining, "The novel that we are going to read is set in this time period. What do we know about the World War II? What would we like to learn more about or what do we wonder about this time or event?"

The students, working in small groups, could fill in the first two columns of the KWL chart and then share their ideas in the large group, or the KWL could be done as a whole-class activity. All ideas offered are respected at this point in the learning. If some feel ideas are given that are inaccurate, they are included nonetheless because the ideas will be revisited after reading and discussing. Later, when the students fill in the *L* column with what they have learned, misinformation and inaccurate facts will be corrected.

Individuals or small groups can provide the information on worksheets, or the class can use a flipchart, art paper, the chalkboard, a transparency, or fill in a large poster that can be referred to and adjusted during the time the novel is being studied.

Anticipation Guides

Another strategy that activates prior knowledge while stimulating interest in what is to be read is the use of an anticipation guide. Like the KWL chart, anticipation guides help readers read to confirm or adjust their predictions, but the anticipation guides work best with nonfiction materials.

K What I Know	W What I Want to Find Out	L What I Have Learned

Figure 6–1 KWL chart

Anticipation guides are a series of statements that are responded to individually before reading and often discussed in groups before the actual reading takes place. This can be done in small groups or as a whole class. This activity raises the expectations about what is to be read.

When preparing anticipation guides, teachers must read the material and write ideas from the text in short declarative sentences. Some of the ideas will be factual ideas from the text, while others will misrepresent what is presented in the text, but each statement must be believable. The statements should be formatted to encourage prediction and anticipation.

Once prepared, the teacher can have the students individually complete the anticipation guide before reading the selection, telling students to make their best guess if they are unsure. The teacher should explain that these guides will not be graded and the students will be free to change any of their answers after reading the selection. After completing the anticipation guide, the teacher and the class discuss the responses and then read the selection independently, if possible, and with a buddy if necessary. The teacher should allow readers to evaluate their predictions, and after reading, discuss their ideas and how their assumptions were confirmed or adjusted.

Anticipation Guide Example: *Bat Loves the Night* **by Nicola Davies**

Choose which you think are true:	Yes	No
1. Bats have toenails.	_____	_____
2. Bats have fur.	_____	_____
3. Bats are blind.	_____	_____
4. Bats have good hearing.	_____	_____
5. Bats make sounds humans can't hear.	_____	_____
6. Most bats eat fish, frogs, or blood.	_____	_____
7. Bats can fly from the time they are born.	_____	_____
8. Bats are mammals.	_____	_____
9. Baby bats are called batties.	_____	_____
10. Bats sleep during the day.	_____	_____

Jackdaws

Teachers know that collections of artifacts related to a book used for class reading or study help stimulate interest in the topic and broaden students' schemas. Such collections of examples are sometimes called *Jackdaws*, which is actually a registered trademark of a company in Amawalk, New York, that supplies collections of hands-on primary source artifacts (similar to the way Kleenex is a product name synonymous with the product itself, tissues). Jackdaws are available from the company at *www.jackdaw.com*, which offers archives of hands-on primary source documents by period, geographical location, or interest. Teachers can begin with these collections or start with their own gleaned from garage sales, flea markets, eBay auctions, and so on, but students should be encouraged to become active in adding to the collection, once they have begun reading a book. Such hunts for related items often involve families as students talk about the Jackdaw at home. For example, during the reading of *Number the Stars* by Lois Lowry, the teacher can begin by sharing maps of Amsterdam and memorabilia from World War II (photos, ration coupons, star flags from windows, newspapers, letters from soldiers/children to parents, and so on). When children talk at home about what they are learning, parents and grandparents will also want to share their treasures, some of which the children can take to class. Sometimes a speaker with firsthand knowledge can be invited to come in and bring in artifacts.

Building background knowledge with such collections helps children understand the time period (setting), the characters, and events. Such hands-on experience makes the reading more real and is often quite helpful to struggling readers who may need a more concrete way to see what's taking place.

There is no limit to what might be collected but teachers might want to consider:

- Maps of the location of the story, showing where it is set or tracing the journey of the character(s)
- Newspapers (real or facsimile) from the time period
- Clothing worn by characters; pictures from books, catalogues, photos, or in some cases, real clothing from secondhand or vintage shops or someone's attic (I still have my father's WWII uniform and many photos of clothing worn in the 1940s.)
- Photos of people or places providing examples of the time period or geographical location
- Songs from the time period, readily available, providing vivid background
- Household items from the time period (I have a box camera from the 1940s, ration books, greeting cards, telegrams, and V-mail [not e-mail])
- Dioramas that illustrate scenes from the book
- Other related books that act as references
- Websites that illustrate information about the time period
- Letters or postcards from the time period

Creating a Scenario

Students sometimes find it difficult to understand content reading that they are unprepared for and lacks authenticity in their purpose for reading. For example, Joe Rubaker, a sixth-grade teacher in Seneca Valley School District in Pennsylvania, finds that reading about the Stamp Act as part of his unit on the American Revolution is difficult for sixth graders because it is so far removed from their lives. Sometimes giving the students a set of circumstances will help readers develop a picture of the situation that will be read about and can create knowledge and interest. This is called creating a scenario—telling a story that contains the elements and conditions that are relevant to the situation. Creating a scenario works well for those who have difficulty with comprehension.

Joe creates a scenario by telling his students that last night he had to go to the store to buy things for his wife. He purchased items that were needed for a wallpapering project that she wanted to begin tomorrow. Joe shopped carefully, paying close attention to prices and items on sale, and he was excited because the total for all the items was $99.00, which was within his planned $100 budget. When Joe went to check out, however, his total bill came to $105—five dollars over budget. Thinking there must be a mistake, Joe went over the cash register receipt with the clerk and found that the six dollars was for tax, something he hadn't budgeted for! Joe was annoyed, and didn't want to pay the store an extra six dollars for nothing, so he went home without the materials. When he got home, his wife wasn't happy with him. Joe asked his class if they thought he did the right thing and why or why not?

Joe says that the discussion that followed gave students a chance to discuss what they knew about taxes, why we have them, how they are used, what is taxed and what isn't, which leads nicely into reading about the Stamp Act, a reading that now has some purpose and connection to their lives.

A Primary Example

The teacher might begin by telling a story about her morning: "I was all ready to go to school and I couldn't find my car keys. I looked on the kitchen counter, on the hook by the door where the keys should have been, and then I started to get nervous. I asked others in the household to help me hunt for them. What do you think were some places we looked? Finally my daughter found them in the pocket of the coat that I had worn the day before and hung in the closet. What a way to start the day!"

The teacher could then ask the students if they have ever hunted for anything and wait for their responses, which could include shoes, Easter eggs, deer, worms, and so on. The teacher could then discuss the different kinds of hunting and why people hunt.

After this discussion, the teacher could introduce *We're Going on a Bear Hunt* to the children by showing them the cover and pointing out the title, author, and illustrator. The teacher could ask who they think the story will probably be about and how they know. "What kind of hunt will these characters be going on? Why do you think so? Let's see what happens."

Guided Imagery/Role Playing

Another strategy that makes use of prior knowledge is guided imagery, sometimes referred to as role playing. The purpose of guided imagery/role playing depends on what text is being used and the teacher's objective. When used as a prereading strategy to create an interest in what would be happening in the story, the teacher sets up a scenario and invites the students to participate. When used as a postreading strategy, the teacher encourages readers to use the text to make connections to their experiences and to confirm or adjust predictions.

As a prereading strategy, the situation or scenario can be presented orally or it can be written and distributed. The scenario is best presented in small groups so all the participants have the opportunity to contribute and a chance to build on others' ideas. After the students have a chance to respond to the scenario or participate in the activity, the whole class can share ideas and responses.

An Intermediate Example

During the reading of *The Cay* by Theodore Taylor, the class can experience what Timothy and Philip felt when they were adrift on a raft in the ocean for days. Before the students enter the room, the teacher, using masking tape on the floor, makes rafts just large enough for two people to fit on (this can be done in the gymnasium or parking lot if more room is needed). Using descriptions from the book, the teacher tells of the feeling of the waves, the danger of sharks, the thirst of the raft occupants, and encourages the students to think about what the characters are experiencing and feeling. Using music of the ocean as a background, the students spend only five minutes on the raft, after which they return quietly to their seats and either write or discuss their experience. After completing that part of the activity, the whole class discusses the experience and connects to the story better by understanding the feelings of the characters.

A Primary Example

After reading *Chester's Way* by Kevin Henkes, before reading the next book on the theme of friendship, the teacher could ask the students to get into groups of four to try the role-playing strategy. One student will pretend to be Chester, Wilson, Lilly, or Victor (who doesn't appear until the last page of the story). The students can role play the day Victor moves into the neighborhood and how the three friends might react to the new addition to the neighborhood. After the groups have a chance to play this through, the teacher can have the whole class discuss what happened in their neighborhoods, how it connected to what happened in the book, and why they decided their interpretation would be reasonable after reading the story.

Brainstorming/Webbing

Brainstorming or webbing is a simple technique that can be used in a variety of ways to stimulate thought and help children make connections. When writing, brainstorming helps children generate ideas for stories and while reading, it can help children in making predictions. Brainstorming can be done in groups or with the whole class; individual readers can also brainstorm, but I've found it works best when participants can build on each other's ideas. The teacher announces the topic and asks the students to tell their group or the class what that topic makes them think of, without evaluating the correctness of the response offered. As words that come to mind about the topic are generated, the teacher, or a student recorder, writes them down in a list, which can then be categorized and arranged, sometimes in webs. For instance, after reading *We're Going on a Bear Hunt,* the children brainstorm what they know about bears. This can lead to a discussion about why the family went on a bear hunt, what they hoped to see, whether they were surprised to see a bear, and why we suppose the family ran away. For example, the following list was brainstormed about bears by kindergarteners:

big	hungry
scary	zoo
brown	black
white	growl
hunt	cubs
woods	furry

The list can then be webbed to help children organize ideas and to form a bridge between prior knowledge and new ideas and vocabulary (see Figure 6–2).

Pretelling/Sequencing

Pretelling is a strategy that supports the sequencing of events and acts as a beginning step to retelling. When comprehending a story, children need to put the pieces of the story together in a sequential or logical order. This requires a type of thinking "backward" (Benson and Cummins 2000, 25). Some children have not yet developed the ability of thinking backward in order to retell a story, so it is helpful to begin with what children already know.

Pretelling involves children consciously thinking about routine events and then thinking backward to the steps that they go through in performing these routines and telling them aloud in a sequential order. Most of these routines are done automatically, and the children have to think about the steps consciously in order to tell them aloud. Lunch routines, lining up in the hall, fire drills, and recess procedures are all routines that can be pretold.

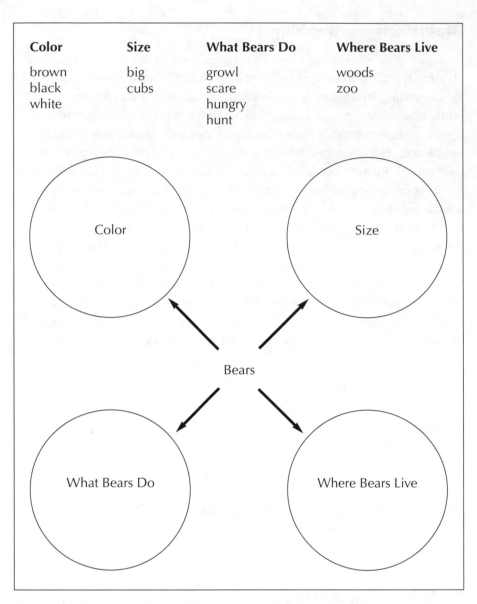

Color	Size	What Bears Do	Where Bears Live
brown	big	growl	woods
black	cubs	scare	zoo
white		hungry	
		hunt	

Figure 6–2 Brainstorming/webbing *We're Going on a Bear Hunt*

Three steps are needed to help children with pretelling: first, identifying the steps in the activity; next, recalling the steps after participating in the event; and last, putting the steps in written form. Using the words *first, next,* and *last* helps the children learn to do this, giving them a framework to organize their thoughts. For example, for recess, *first* we put away our work, *next* we get our coats, and *last* we line up quietly at the door. At recess time the teacher can ask the class to verbally go over the steps, and then she can use a chart to write them out for review. This repetition using the words *first, next,* and *last* with routines helps children begin to recall things in order, a precursor to retelling. After using pretelling for routine activities, teachers can use this technique with instructional activities, such as figuring out unknown words or deciding how to solve a math problem (Benson and Cummins 2000, 27).

As with most instructional strategies, modeling is essential in this process. Teachers should begin by teaching pretelling *to* children, then move to pretelling *with* children, and eventually expect pretelling to be done by children *themselves*. Some suggestions of activities to use to model pretelling events include:

morning routines

checking out a library book

taking lunch count

calendar and weather reports

morning message

clean up time

how to make an art activity

how to regroup in math

asking for help

lavatory procedure

figuring out an unknown word

using the computer

Inferential Strategy

Inferential strategy models how readers predict before reading and during reading, and it can provide support as children learn to develop predicting and inferencing abilities during the reading of a story (Hansen 1981). The inferential strategy procedure, which be used in a whole- or small-group situation, works like this:

1. The teacher analyzes a story to be used for the important ideas in the text. Before having the children read the selection, the teacher chooses three ideas that are seen as most important to the theme of the story.
2. The teacher plans prereading questions, two questions for each of the three ideas. One of the questions should activate prior knowledge that relates to the story and the other question should be a prediction question. For example, if a teacher were using the story *Chester's Way* by Kevin Henkes, the pair of questions might be:
    a. What is a best friend? (prior knowledge/background)
    b. In this part of the story you are going to meet two mice named Chester and Wilson who are best friends. What are some things you think best friends might do together? (prediction)

        Students are encouraged to write their predictions (or draw as a form of writing, whichever is more developmentally appropriate). This way, time is given to thinking of an answer, and each child is predicting, instead of only one or two children volunteering. Then a discussion of predictions can take place, in the next step.

3. Before reading the selection, the teacher and students discuss background and prediction responses.

4. The teacher and students read the entire story or a part of the story. This can be done aloud to the group, silently by each individual, in small groups, or with buddies.

5. After reading, the teacher and students discuss how student predictions related to the actual events in the story. They discuss the three ideas that motivated the background and prediction questions. For example, to continue with *Chester's Way,* the three basic ideas of the story, as identified by the teacher, were:

    ■ Best friends like to do things together.
    ■ People who are different can teach us new things.
    ■ We're all alike and different in some ways.

With these ideas in mind, the background questions could include: We've all met people who are like us and sometimes we meet people who are different. Perhaps they come from another country, or live in the city, or have a big family when we have only one sister. When we get to know this new person, can they teach us anything new? The prediction elements could include: The characters in this story meet a new person in their neighborhood named Lilly who seems very different from them. How do you think they will react? Will they be her friend?

Children have a great deal of experience, even in primary grades, with making friends and have much to contribute to this discussion. At the end of the story, another character is introduced, Victor, and the children can continue their predictions in writing, based on what they have learned about the relationship between Chester and Wilson and Lilly.

CHAPTER SEVEN

During Reading

Procedures to Support Comprehension

Accomplished readers use a variety of strategies, such as imagery, predicting, and self-questioning, to bring meaning to what they are reading, techniques that less proficient readers need to learn. Again, the best way to teach these strategies is not to tell the children or to list them, but to model them as part of our shared reading sessions. This modeling is similar to another strategy discussed later in the chapter—thinking aloud, during which a teacher shares with the children what he does when reading.

Strategies to Use During Reading

It isn't necessary to use the terms for the strategies applied during reading with the children, such as looking for context clues; it's the procedures that you want them to understand and eventually internalize.

Imagery. A proficient reader sees the actions in the story in her mind's eye as she reads. When I was young, I could see Nancy Drew zipping along in her red roadster with Ned at her side. I could see that spooky old house and the mysterious old grandfather clock (although at that time in my life, I think the only experience I had with grandfather clocks was in pictures, like the one on the paper cover of my book). The words on the page formed pictures for me, and I got lost in the story. Such imagery helps readers comprehend. Asking children what they are seeing in their heads helps, as does drawing and sharing. Older children can use response logs to share their images as they read.

Predicting. Teachers need to help children predict as they read. Teachers can begin by simply asking, "What do you think might happen next?" with very young children and this strategy can continue throughout the grades. For example, if reading the story *Something from Nothing*, the teacher can ask, "After making a vest from a jacket, what do you think the grandfather will make next? After we've made a variety of predictions, based on what we know about the size of the items, we'll read on to see if we're correct." Again, proficient readers are always making, adjusting, and confirming their predictions as they read, and we need to model this strategy for beginning or developing readers.

Self-Questioning. When reading, readers need to ask, "Does this make sense to me?" "Is this what I thought would happen?" "Is this connecting with what I've already read?" Such questions will help readers read to predict or confirm, and help readers learn to direct their own reading experience. Such questioning is much more valuable to comprehension than the teacher's questions that "test" comprehension. Self-questioning helps readers learn to take control of the reading experience. Teachers must model self-questioning, encourage readers to use it, and take time to ask students about the questions they posed to themselves.

Context Clues, Rereading, and Skipping. It's important to help students see that proficient readers use the cues of context, both semantic and syntactic, to help them figure out what words mean. Sometimes it's okay to skip the word and read on, but other times, it helps a reader to stop, reread, and try to figure out unknown words. The important thing to learn is when it makes a difference and that the purpose is to make sense or get meaning. Word-perfect reading is more important in primary grades because text is short and most words used are important to the meaning. When texts get longer, readers should learn when it's efficient to skip rather than reread and that sometimes context clues are found as the text continues. Thinking aloud about how you read and figure out difficult words helps to model this strategy for developing readers. When working with readers during guided reading (discussed later), teachers should include discussion about context clues, rereading and skipping and how these decisions were made.

Adjusting Reading Rate. Adjusting one's reading rate doesn't necessarily mean slowing down. Proficient readers learn to adjust their reading rate to help them make meaning. As a reader, sometimes I slow down when I'm reading a part that is difficult, confusing, extremely important to the story, and so on. However, I sometimes speed up, perhaps if the writer's long descriptions are interfering with my meaning making or if I sense what is coming up will help me better understand what I am reading. Teachers need to model these strategies for readers; however, telling children to slow down is often not the answer. Slowing down can actually interfere with comprehension because it interferes with constructing the thread of meaning (Simon 1974; F. Smith 1994). Instead, slow down and reread, and then read on if it still seems difficult, is better advice.

Paraphrasing (Summarizing). Proficient readers do not consciously use paraphrasing as a strategy very often, although when beginning a new chapter or when resuming reading after setting a book down for a day or so, readers do rehearse in their heads what has happened so far in the story. Younger readers, to see if they understand what they are reading, can try this as they go along and also use the time to make predictions. This is more frequently done with longer selections or in discussion groups, such as literature circles (discussed in detail later in this chapter), to help the participants with conversation.

Asking for Help. When all other strategies have failed, readers ask for help. Even adult readers, for example in book clubs, ask questions, such as, "I didn't understand why he reacted the way he did on page 201. Did I miss something?" It is important that readers learn to be independent, but they must also see that it's appropriate to ask questions and to take risks. Sometimes meaning is best made with the help of another reader.

Comprehension Strategy Framework

Most teachers want to teach children to become strategic readers but are often at a loss as to how to best teach this skill. The comprehension strategy framework, a successful format for teaching comprehension, gives students an understanding of how proficient readers use strategies such as prediction, use of background knowledge, and analyzing the text visually. The framework, developed by Sarah Dowhower (1999), focuses on three phases of interactive teaching, which occur during prereading, active reading, and postreading. This framework focuses on themes or big issues in comprehension and can be used to teach any story.

The comprehension strategy framework might be set up as follows (and an example in Figure 7–1 illustrates how the components are applied in a lesson using the trade book *Owl Moon*):

- **Prereading.** The teacher will find ways to:
  a. elicit students' prior knowledge
  b. build background and relate that to prior knowledge
  c. focus on the specific strategy to be taught—what the strategy is and why it is being taught
- **Active Reading.** During the actual reading of the text (orally or silently), the teacher finds ways to:
  a. set a purpose for reading specific section of text
  b. encourage students to silent read and self-monitor
  c. "work the story" (Encourage discussion that helps children become part of what they have read.) This shouldn't seem like an interroga-

tion, but the discussion should include continuous personal demonstrations and naming of strategies, for example, "I found myself doing _____ in order to understand this."

    d. encourage students to repeat active reading phase until end of selection

    e. pull the story together through a final discussion for the construction of themes (thinking on higher levels; the big idea)

- **Postreading** (individually or in groups; choose one or more according to need and appropriateness). This can be supported through various activities such as discussion, response logs, mapping, writing, role playing, and so on (see Chapter 8).

    a. recall of content

    b. reader response

    c. extensions of text

    d. strategy use and transfer

    e. informal or self-assessment

Reciprocal Teaching

Reciprocal teaching helps students think strategically about reading and understand text by providing a model of proficient reading. During a reading, the teacher raises questions about the reading, makes predictions, summarizes, and clarifies vocabulary and ideas (Palincsar and Brown 1984). In another version of this activity, reciprocal questioning or ReQuest (Manzo 1969), students learn to ask their own questions. A simple reciprocal teaching procedure based on both forms of this strategy might be organized as follows:

1. The teacher divides the passage to be read into fairly short sections (one or two paragraphs at a time; for longer selections, several pages may be included).
2. The teacher asks students to read the section silently. The reading can be read ahead to provide time for slower readers and the second reading at this time can act as a review.
3. After reading, the teacher models the comprehension process by following these four steps:
   a. *Summarize* the section in one or two sentences.
   b. *Ask* the group one or two good questions, avoiding picky details.
   c. *Identify* a difficult part of the passage and *clarify it* by explaining, giving examples, drawing analogies, or making clarifying statements.
   d. *Predict* what the next section might be about, or what might be learned from it.
4. The teacher should repeat steps 1 through 3 until the pattern is familiar to students. Afterward, she can take turns leading the discussion steps: teacher-student-teacher-student, or teacher-student-student-student, and so on. The teacher's modeling and continued involvement is critical to the students' success with the procedure.

Here's an example of reciprocal teaching, using Chapter 2 of *Gathering Blue* by Lois Lowry (appropriate for fifth or sixth grade):

Framework Components	The Lesson (Teacher's remarks and comments)
	Prereading
Prediction— Story elements	Today we're going to read a book called *Owl Moon* by Jane Yolen and illustrated by John Schoenherr. By looking at the cover, whom do you think this story is about? What time of year is it? What time of day? Where are they? (setting) This book has a seal on the cover that tells us that it won an award called the Caldecott Medal for its wonderful illustrations. This means that the pictures in the book will also tell us a lot about the story.
Elicit prior knowledge	Have any of you ever walked in the woods with a parent or grandparent? At night? Why?
Build background	This story is about a boy and his dad going "owling." What do you think that might be?
Introduce strategies that will be used #1 #2	How can we figure this out as we're reading? How can we figure out what owling is if we've never done it? We can use a reading strategy where we use what we do know (about woods, animals, hunting, etc.) to connect to something new in order to understand it. We can also try to organize the story in our heads so we can understand it better. After reading today, we'll use a story map to do this (mapping needs to be taught in previous lesson).
	Active Reading
Set purpose	As we read this story, we'll learn what owling is, what an owl moon is, and decide if it's something we might enjoy. I'll read the first few pages to introduce you to the characters and what they are doing.
Story elements	(Read out loud.) After students share ideas about the setting, the teacher might ask, How do we know? Then the teacher continues, How do you think the boy feels?
Set purpose	Let's read the next couple of pages silently to find out what the dad and boy do when they "owl." Please read to the bottom of page X and stop.
Demonstrate *my* use of a strategy	You know, after I read this part, I realized the boy had older brothers. How do you think I knew this? What did you learn? Please continue reading to page X.
Demonstrate importance of language/ words to comprehend	(After reading that part) I loved the sentences where the author used descriptive words or phrases to help me see, hear, and feel what the boy was experiencing. Can anyone find any of these words or phrases?
Purpose for activity	(Read the next part.) Now continue reading the story silently. When you're finished, organize the story by using the story map in preparation for our group discussion. (The teacher will have given the students a story map with a familiar format, perhaps the "Someone-Wants-But-So" format; see Chapter 8).
	Postreading
Discussion, not interrogation	(Students will begin by sharing responses to map. The teacher will lead discussion with questions that promote discussion, rather than ones that feel like cross-examination.)
Recall Inference	What did the boy know about owling? Why did he say you have to be brave?
Connect to personal experience	How do you think the boy felt when he saw an owl? How do you think he would have felt if he hadn't seen an owl? How is this story like an experience you've had?
Reader response	I loved the last page. Let's read it aloud again.
Theme "big idea"	Take a few minutes and write in your response journal about what you think the author could have meant in this last page, and we'll talk about your ideas when we're finished.
Review strategies used	(Share.) What strategies did we use to understand this story better? ■ We predicted ■ We looked at how the author used descriptive words to help us understand ■ We connected to our own experiences ■ We used visuals (a map) to help us organize the story in our head.

Figure 7–1 Example of a comprehension strategy lesson for *Owl Moon*

1. The teacher prereads the chapter and decides on appropriate stopping points.
2. The students read the first two pages of the chapter silently.
3. After reading:
   a. *Summarize* by saying "Kira returns to her village after her mother's death hoping to find a place for herself in the community. She sees her recently widowed uncle and his two children who seem to ignore her."
   b. *Ask* questions—"What do you think is Kira's most important need at this time? What do you think about the ways families behave in this culture?"
   c. *Clarify* (a difficult part: "Pleasantries were not a part of their custom.")—"I would infer that this means that manners and greeting people and blessing them when they sneezed were not part of what these people were taught."
   d. *Make predictions*—"Let's read on to find out what Kira does first." Or, "I think we might find out who helps her."
4. Repeat steps *a* through *d* with the second part of the chapter:
   a. *Summarize* by saying, "Kira is hungry but there is little left at her burned-down home. Her mother's garden is being stripped by thieves and the vegetables are essential to Kira's nourishment, since there is no man in her life to hunt for meat. We also meet Vandara, who is introduced in Chapter 1 as the ringleader in Kira's trouble. The description of the woman is frightening, especially the scar caused by the beasts."
   b. *Ask questions*—"Why can't Kira hunt for meat?" and "How do others feel about Vandara?"
   c. *Clarify*—"Today, facing Kira, she once again prepares to destroy someone's young" refers to the rumor or tale of Vandara killing. . . . Today she is preparing to kill Kira, a young orphan."
   d. *Make predictions*—"In this next part we may find out why Vandara wants Kira killed and how Kira will respond to Vandara."

Guided Reading

Guided reading is a model of instruction that gives teachers opportunities to support young readers as they grow and lead them to independent reading (see Figure 7–2). The New Zealand Department of Education believes, "Guided reading enables children to practice strategies with the teacher's support and leads to independent silent reading" (quoted in Fountas and Pinnell 1996, 1). Guided reading serves several purposes (Fountas and Pinnell 1996, 1). It

- Gives students the opportunity to develop as individual readers in a small group that supports them.
- Gives teachers a way to assess students as they read texts at their instructional level.

	Before the reading	During the reading	After the reading
Teacher	• selects an appropriate text, one that will be supportive but with a few problems to solve • prepares an introduction to the story • briefly introduces the story, keeping in mind the meaning, language, and visual information in the text, and the knowledge, experience, and skills of the reader • leaves some questions to be answered through reading	• "listens in" • observes the reader's behaviors for evidence of strategy use • confirms children's problem-solving attempts and successes • interacts with individuals to assist with problem solving at difficulty (when appropriate) • makes notes about the strategy use of individual readers	• talks about the story with the children • invites personal response • returns to the text for one or two teaching opportunities such as finding evidence or discussing problem solving • assesses children's understanding of what they read • sometimes engages the children in extending the story through such activities as drama, writing, art, or more reading
Children	• engage in a conversation about the story • raise questions • build expectations • notice information in the text	• read the whole text or a unified part to themselves (softly or silently) • request help in problem solving when needed	• talk about the story • check predictions and react personally to the story or information • revisit the text at points of problem solving as guided by the teacher • may reread the story to a partner or independently • sometimes engage in activities that involve extending and responding to the text (such as drama or journal writing)

Figure 7–2 Essential elements of guided reading

- Gives readers a chance to develop strategic reading habits that help them develop into independent readers.
- Provides an enjoyable low-risk reading situation for children.
- Helps students learn to know how to approach the reading of unfamiliar texts.

Irene Fountas and Gay Su Pinnell (1996) outline the essential elements of guided reading in Figure 7–2.

Literature Circles

Literature circles can be a part of a reading program at any grade level. Literature circles, simply put, are a group of three to five readers who gather to discuss a book they are reading or have read. The students guide the discussions and the discussions are in-depth responses to the students' reading. These groups are minicommunities that encourage personal response to what is being read as they construct meaning from the text and negotiate that meaning with others in their group. Discussion may center on characters, plot development, the author's writing style, or personal connections to the story itself. Literature circles provide an opportunity for participants to think critically about what they have read and to gain a deeper understanding by sharing their understandings.

For literature circles to be truly student-centered, they must involve student choice, personal response, and responsibility (Noe and Johnson 1999). They are not teacher-led with questions meant to check student understandings. Rather, literature circles are similar to what adults do when they gather to discuss a favorite book in someone's home over cake and coffee: the group chooses a book they want to read (based on recommendations, the *New York Times'* Best Sellers list, and so on), they decide by what date they will have it read, and they gather to share their own personal interpretations, questions, and connections. In the process of discussion, they negotiate understanding, reread for more in-depth analysis, and discuss their personal reactions to the book and the writing style. This is what real readers do and such experiences can be a part of classroom reading experiences through literature circles.

Choosing Books and Forming Groups. Books chosen for literature circles should promote discussion and student choice is best if we want children to be interested and have ownership. It's understandable that teachers have a limited set of books, but teachers should work to provide choice with what is available. For instance, after introducing five different possibilities, the student can list his first, second, and third choice of the five. Such a system still allows for student choice, but it also enables the teacher to group students appropriately (groups should be heterogeneous and varied throughout the year).

Introducing Books. Children will choose books with more enthusiasm if teachers spend time creating interest before asking them to choose. Informal book talks should pique students' curiosity and entice them without telling too much or giving away the plot. Reading a short part aloud gives the students a sense of the author's writing style and a mental image of the setting. It's also interesting to have a student who has already read the book give the book talk, but make sure you help with this or model several talks before asking a student to do one. You can even invite a student from a higher grade to visit and share his experience with the book.

Giving book talks in the morning, or even the day before students are to make their choice, gives students a chance to look at and consider the books. In addition to choosing based on knowing something of the story itself, students need to see how the books are written, chapter length, and print size. Teachers should honor students' choices and support them even when their choice is on a somewhat difficult level (a list of professional books offering ideas to support challenged readers in literature circles is found at the end of this discussion on page 110).

How Much to Read and When to Read.

How literature circle books are read depends on the age and reading development of the participants. Primary students typically read picture books that can be read or reread in one sitting; some teachers send these books home to be read, others find time and assistance to make sure all students have an adult read with them before circle time. When students are ready for simple chapter books, which seems to be a right of passage for many first and second graders, teachers can suggest reading a chapter a day and preparing that chapter for discussion. When students are ready for literature with longer chapters, the teacher can turn some of the decision making over to the students, with participants in the circles dividing the book according to their needs, keeping in mind the time limit the teacher has set for completion of the book and discussion. Older readers who are struggling should be provided with assistance, either from an adult, such as an aid or resource room teacher, or a reading partner. Challenged readers can also read along with some of the excellent literature available on tape or CD (both audio CD and computer CD-ROM), or their teachers might even make their own taped readings. The important thing is that all readers have an enjoyable reading experience and are reading to add their ideas to the discussion during circle time.

Structure of Discussion Groups.

Students of all ages need to learn to discuss what they read. Simply putting children together in groups and asking them to discuss without any instruction will be a disaster. Conversely, taking over a literature circle with teacher questions and answers will also be a disappointing experience for all involved. Figure 7–3 provides a chart to help teachers make decisions based on purpose and objectives (Noe and Johnson 1999, 19).

Teaching Students How to Discuss.

Literature circles resonate with the voices of each member of the group working to deepen understanding and appreciation of a story, but learning how to discuss and to achieve such an

Format	Teacher Role	Benefits	Challenges
One group meets at a time; other students work on reading, journal writing, extension projects	Facilitator	Control Opportunity to teach strategies for conversation and response May be an easier format for beginning literature circles	Students tend to talk to teacher, not each other Students not in discussion need to be able to work independently
One group meets at a time	Group member	Control Opportunity to model conversation and response Also a manageable format for beginning literature circles	Students tend to talk to teacher, not each other Students not in discussion need to be able to work independently
One group meets at a time	Removed observer	Control Opportunity to observe students' growth in discussion and response	Teacher's observation needs to be unobtrusive so that conversation is not stifled Students not in discussion need to be able to work independently
Two or more groups meet at a time	Observer and guide	Flexibility Opportunity to observe students' growth in discussion and response Greater input for discussion debriefings	Greater noise levels Teacher has less opportunity for in-depth assessment Possibility for chaos, unproductive behavior

Figure 7–3 Variations for discussions

outcome takes practice and support from an expert; discussion requires much modeling and teaching. Teachers may find the following ideas helpful as they teach students how to discuss, and the recommended professional books listed at the end of this section will provide additional resources.

Post-It notes can be used while reading to mark pages that readers will want to discuss when they are in their groups. Primary children, given five sticky notes, will choose their favorite parts, funny parts, parts that remind them of something else, or pages with new or challenging words. Older students, who are given a pack of small sticky notes, use them to remind themselves of parts that surprise, confuse, connect with something they've done or read, add new vocabulary, and so on. As students share what they have marked, they discover new uses for their notes.

Role sheets have been used successfully in all grades. As explained in detail by Harvey Daniels in his book *Literature Circles: Voice and Choice in Book Clubs and Reading Groups* (2002), role sheets contain task instructions that students use in order to prepare for discussion. Each member of the group chooses a role from the following: questioner, connector, illustrator, summarizer, passage picker, researcher, word wizards, and so on. (See Appendix E for sample role sheets based on Daniels' book.) These roles focus readers' attention on a single responsibility and teach them to involve every person in the discussion. These role sheets are used until the teacher and students feel that they have a good idea of how to prepare and facilitate their discussions, and then teachers wean students away from role sheets and demonstrate the use of other methods to prepare for discussion, including sticky notes or response logs.

Quotes and questions can be used in conjunction with sticky notes, role sheets, or journals. Students are asked to choose one quote they would like to discuss and think about why they thought it was important, and identify one question they have as a reader about that section of the reading. This works well when teachers have modeled their own thinking while reading with real reader questions instead of teacher questions. If students ask generic questions like, "What was the setting?" instead of ones responding to the story, such as, "I wonder why he lied in the first place?" teachers may find it worthwhile to model questions that are outgrowths of making meaning rather than ones that "check comprehension."

Prompts are often used in response logs or journals to help students react and reflect. Prompts can be used with primary students as discussion starters. I've even written prompts on strips of paper and put them in a basket in the middle of the table, from which we chose at random to start things off. Some of my favorites include:

I wonder . . .

I think . . .

I liked the part where . . .

One of my questions is . . .

The most interesting/surprising/funniest part was . . .

I predict that . . .

I could connect with the part where . . .

If I were _____, I would . . .

Journals and logs, popular tools for readers to use in intermediate grades, can be used to give students an opportunity to reflect on what they have read, similar to the work they did with role sheets. Of course, such reflection takes time to learn and must be modeled by the teacher. Other formats for logs can be more structured, with the reader filling in a prepared format after each part of the reading. Figure 7–4 gives a sample format.

Bookmarks are used to gather information while reading. Like Post-It notes, bookmarks help students identify parts they want to discuss,

Title _____ Author _____

Date of Discussion _____ Pages to Discuss _____

Interesting Vocabulary (word and page) _____

The part I wanted to discuss with my group was on page_____, paragraph _____, because

_____

_____

_____

_____

_____

_____

One question I have about the reading or about what we will read next is

_____

_____

_____

_____

_____

_____

_____

_____

Figure 7–4 Literature circle log format

```
┌─────────────────────────────┐
│                             │
│   NAME of the STORY         │
│                             │
│                             │
│   My name _____   │
│                             │
│   Date _____    │
│                             │
│   Title _____    │
│                             │
│   Pages _____    │
│                             │
│                             │
│                             │
│   New, interesting, or hard words: │
│                             │
│                             │
│   _____  _____    │
│                             │
│   _____  _____    │
│                             │
│   _____  _____    │
│                             │
│   _____  _____    │
│                             │
│                             │
│                             │
│   Questions, ideas: _____ │
│                             │
│                             │
│   _____   │
│                             │
│   _____   │
│                             │
│   _____   │
│                             │
│   _____   │
│                             │
│   _____   │
│                             │
│                             │
└─────────────────────────────┘
```

Figure 7–5 Sample literature circle bookmark

questions they may have while reading, and unfamiliar words they encounter while reading. On a bookmark slip of paper, teachers can prepare a guide similar to the sample bookmark shown in Figure 7–5, which students can complete and then bring to their discussion group.

Other forms of response depend on the particular reading selection. The important thing to remember is that activities should be meaningful and not just exercises or time fillers. Depending on the selection, a variety of ideas can stimulate response, such as diary entries, cause and effect charts, letters, illustrations, character or story maps, and dialogue journals (Noe and Johnson 1999).

Teachers must be selective about what type of tools and strategies they use. If students were to try all of these ideas, there would be no time for real discussion. Try different ideas with different books and use what seems best for your particular grade level and group of students.

Assessing and Evaluating Literature Circles. Literature circles are not graded in the traditional sense of giving tests and quizzes as students read, but because they take a great deal of class and instructional time and are an integral part of a reading program, teachers have the responsibility of knowing how children are progressing and can often use assessment tools for reporting reading growth to parents.

Because several literature circles may meet simultaneously and the teacher cannot be present during all of them, teachers need strategies to assess the progress of the individual students as they read and partici-pate. Anecdotal records are quite helpful, especially when the teacher has an opportunity to sit in on the circle and actually observe what is hap-pening. Checklists can be used by the teacher to record observations or even by adult volunteers who are sitting in on literature circles (see Fig-ure 7–6). If these checklists are maintained over a period of time, the teacher will be able to gather enough data to form a picture of what is happening in literature circles, allowing assessment of students' strengths and needs.

Self-assessment is an important part of assessment procedures in classes using literature circles. Such assessments help students take responsibility for their own reading, discussion, participation, and learning. Examples of self-assessments that can be used are shown in Figures 7–7, 7–8, and 7–9.

Recommended Professional Books. Teachers who wish a more com-plete treatment of literature circles and further help with implementing them in the classroom may find the following references excellent:

- *Getting Started with Literature Circles* by Katherine Schlick Noe and Nancy Johnson
- *Literature Circles and Response* by Bonnie Campbell Hill, Nancy Johnson, and Katherine Schlick Noe
- *Literature Circles Resource Guide* by Bonnie Campbell Hill, Katherine Schlick Noe, and Nancy Johnson
- *Literature Circles: Voice and Choice in Book Clubs and Reading Groups* by Harvey Daniels
- *Mini-Lessons for Literature Circles* by Harvey Daniels and Nancy Steineke

Directed Reading-Thinking Activity (DRTA)

The directed reading-thinking activity (DRTA), a problem-solving discussion strategy, provides students with a framework for working through a text

Name of observer (if other than teacher) _____

Title of book _____ Date _____

Observed Response	**Student Names**				
Seems to enjoy book					
Participates in discussion					
Has prepared for discussion					
Draws conclusions					
Makes predictions					
Explains responses					
Uses text to support ideas					
Makes connections					
Thoughtful listener					
Polite responder					

Observer's comments:

Figure 7–6 Observation checklist for literature circle response

Name _____ Date _____

Title of book _____

I read the agreed-upon number of pages.   ☐ Yes   ☐ Most of them   ☐ Few or no pages

I wrote in my response journal.   ☐ Yes   ☐ Briefly   ☐ No

I participated in circle discussion.   ☐ Yes   ☐ Somewhat   ☐ Little or no

I was a thoughtful participant.   ☐ Yes   ☐ Sometimes   ☐ No

Figure 7–7 Self-evaluation for literature circle response

Name _____ Date _____

Title of book _____

In literature circle today, I did the following well (include reflection concerning your participation, risk taking, questioning, expanding on another's thought or idea, connecting with experiences in your life or with other books you've read, encouraging other's ideas and responses):

_____

_____

_____

In future literature circle meetings, I plan to:

_____

_____

_____

_____

In order to accomplish this, I will:

_____

_____

_____

_____

Figure 7–8 Narrative self-evaluation for literature circle response

Name _____ Date _____

Title of book _____

My participation in today's discussion was (check one): ☐ good ☐ satisfactory ☐ poor

What led you to this evaluation (examples of your participation)?

_____

Our group's discussion today was (check one): ☐ good ☐ satisfactory ☐ poor

An important idea that emerged from today's discussion was:

_____

Contributions of other group members were (include names of members):

_____

_____

_____

Our plans for our next meeting include:

_____

_____

_____

Figure 7–9 Today's literature circle evaluation and reflection

and using strategies that will aid in comprehension by improving reading and thinking skills (Stauffer 1980). This strategy can be used with both fiction and nonfiction, with trade books and basal stories.

During a DRTA lesson, students move through phases of hypothesizing, validating or rejecting, and modifying original ideas. The first step involves asking students to make predictions about the story based on the title and any cover or cover page illustrations. This prediction requires students to use their background knowledge and experience. It also gives students a place to begin when reading. Students then read silently to a point predetermined by the teacher, who asks questions that facilitate discussion and helps the students decide if their initial predictions were accurate, or to adjust them accordingly. The teacher encourages the students to return to the text to confirm their answers to questions. At this point, the students make new predictions, read to the next predetermined point, and repeat the discussion process.

Suggested Procedure

1. Looking at the title of a book, or illustrations if available, students make initial predictions about what the story or text will be about. These predictions will be determined by the students' individual schemas (background knowledge) and can be used with individual students or with students as a group.
2. Once predictions are made, students read to points in the story predetermined by the teacher. After each stopping point, the teacher leads discussion encouraging the students to confirm or adjust their original projections, using the text to support their ideas.
3. Following each discussion of previous predictions, the students make predictions about what is to come next and continue reading to the next predetermined point. This pattern of predicting, confirming or modifying, looking for support from the text to support ideas, and making further predictions continues until the end of the selection or until an appropriate place to invite students to finish the selection on their own.

Teacher Preparation. The teacher's role in the DRTA includes prereading the selection to determine stopping points and where to pose questions to initiate discussion as well as to keep discussion going. These questions are not at the literal level, but are more interpretive. For example, typical questions for predictions can begin by simply asking, "What do you think this story is going to be about?" and "What makes you think this?" After reading a section the teacher might ask, "Were our predictions accurate?" "Did you expect the character to act this way?" and "Did anything in this part of the story surprise you?" Before continuing with the reading, the teacher might ask, "What do you think is going to happen?" and "What part of the story makes you think this?" The teacher can return to the reading by saying, "Well, let's continue reading to see if our predictions are correct."

The goal in teacher questioning in a DRTA is not to elicit answers the teacher might feel are correct, but for the teacher to say as little as possible to get the students thinking about the story.

Using DRTA with struggling readers has many benefits. For example, the voices in the discussion analyzing the story are the students', not the teacher's; having an opportunity to predict based on the story so far seems to help students construct understanding, and the activity promotes students taking responsibility for their own learning.

Think-Alouds

Thinking aloud is a process in which a reader verbalizes her own thoughts that occur when reading a story. Think-alouds can help teachers understand how students read by giving access to their thought processes. Think-aloud procedures usually begin with a teacher modeling the process, demonstrating to students what is happening as she reads, and what decisions she is making and why, which gives the children an example of the thought processes a proficient reader uses when she is reading.

The procedure for modeling think-alouds begins with the teacher selecting a challenging passage to read (Hinson 2000). This passage should contain unknown vocabulary, ambiguities, or areas in which the reader is forced to make decisions or predictions. The teacher reads the text aloud and the student(s) follow along silently.

The teacher then chooses areas where comprehension is not obviously clear and stops to explain how he is figuring out what is happening. Some examples of the types of behavior to model might be:

- Tell students when you are making predictions (developing hypotheses). This can happen as early as the title by looking at the cover, the words in the title, or the heading. Readers also make predictions throughout the text. Stop and explain what might happen. Explain when predictions are confirmed and how they are adjusted when new information is added: "I think this story is going to be about a boy and his dog, who is named Shiloh," or "I was wrong about his going to his dad; I think this will cause him even more trouble. Let's see."
- Describe what you are seeing as you read (developing images). "I picture this boy's home to be really poor, but neat and clean. I think of TV shows like *The Waltons*, with a farm and lots of land in the mountains, but not many material things."
- Make connections to what you know (link prior knowledge to new information). "This reminds me of when I wanted a dog, but my circumstances were different. I wanted the dog, but my parents were not against it. We also didn't have much money, but we weren't as poor as this family was. I do understand wanting a dog badly."
- Verbalize areas of confusion or words you don't understand (monitoring ongoing comprehension). "This isn't what I thought he would do. I don't understand why he would change his mind and give the dog to the boy."

It's difficult to model how we figure out challenging vocabulary because we understand the vocabulary of the texts we are reading with children. I don't pretend to not know a word—children know that you can read, but you can say that you think a particular word might be challenging for them, and a way you'd figure it out would be to skip it and see if you needed it, or look for smaller words in this word, or ask if it looks like a word you know, and so on.

■ Demonstrate how you make sense of what you are reading (how you help yourself with comprehension; how you use multiple strategies). Explain when you need to reread and why. Sometimes you may need to read ahead to see if what you are predicting makes sense or if you can make sense of the new vocabulary.

In order to model think-alouds, the teacher must read the selection ahead of time and plan the instruction. Proficient readers do many of these things automatically and they need to stop and think about what they do so they can verbalize it. After the teacher models think-alouds, students can work with a partner and practice thinking aloud about what they are reading. When students are beginning this process, the materials that they use should be selected by the teacher with obvious opportunities to talk about strategies. Using a simple model such as the one shown in Figure 7–10, students have a format to use as they begin to think about their own reading.

There are various ways to assess think-alouds. One useful resource is *Portfolios and Beyond: Collaborative Assessment in Reading and Writing* by Susan Mandel Glazer and Carol Brown (1993). Basically, the teacher can:

■ Take notes (anecdotal records) as the child thinks aloud
■ Tape-record the session and analyze what was happening, either alone or along with the student
■ Use a checklist or rubric, paying specific attention to the student's predicting, connecting, characterization, summarizing, reacting, picturing, inferencing, rereading, and use of all three cueing systems (semantic, syntactic, graphic cues).

Students can also self-assess while thinking aloud, using a checklist such as one adapted from Dorothy Strickland and Lesley Morrow (1990) (see Figure 7–10).

Shared Reading

Shared reading is one of the most valuable tools a teacher of reading can employ in a small-group or whole-class situation. Simply put, shared reading is the process of being able to participate in a literature experience by having the literature read to a group by a teacher (or another trained adult). The procedure resembles the reading of a bedtime story in which the child can see the book and participate along with the adult reader. Don Holdaway (1980) discusses three stages in shared reading:

1. **Discovery**. The reading selection is introduced with the purpose of enjoying a literary experience.

Check the activities you used.

	Yes	Sometimes	No
I made pictures in my mind.	_____	_____	_____
I made predictions looking at the title and pictures.	_____	_____	_____
I asked myself questions as I read.	_____	_____	_____
I went back and reread the parts that didn't make sense.	_____	_____	_____
I stopped and talked about ideas in the story.	_____	_____	_____
I connected the story to things I am familiar with.	_____	_____	_____
I figured out unfamiliar words by how they were used in the story.	_____	_____	_____
I made predictions as I read.	_____	_____	_____
I connected what I knew to new information from the story.	_____	_____	_____
I talked about confusing parts.	_____	_____	_____
I used appropriate strategies when I became confused.	_____	_____	_____

Think-Aloud

I think that _____

I wonder _____

I'm confused about _____

This reminds me of _____

Now I understand why _____

Figure 7–10 A think-aloud checklist

2. **Exploration.** The selection is reread or looked at more deeply. It is during this stage that children discover ideas about how readers read, looking at how stories come together, and strategies that proficient readers use to make sense of print.
3. **Independent experience and expression.** Students use what they have read to engage in connected reading and writing experiences.

Conducting a Shared Reading Session. The primary purpose of shared reading is the enjoyment of literature. Any teacher or other adult sharing a reading experience with a child should attend to the following:

1. **Choosing the selection.** It's always most appropriate to have the students choose the selection to be read, as small children do during bedtime story time. However, the adult can also introduce a new story to readers, as parents often do. Both experiences are important in a classroom.
2. **The teacher introduces the selection** (book, story, chart, poem) using a combination of appropriate strategies:
   - discussing the cover of the book, including title, author, and illustrators
   - activating prior knowledge, connecting to what students already know about the topic, characters, setting, and so on
   - making predictions, asking what the students think this story may be about and why they think that
   - connecting to other books
   - previewing the text, doing a picture walk for picture books, looking at length of chapters and selections for intermediate readers (For intermediate readers, reading the back cover and discussing it are ways to preview the text.)
3. **The adult or teacher reads through the text,** without pausing if the selection is short, or pausing and providing time for students to:
   - predict what might happen
   - confirm or adjust predictions
   - discuss illustrations or connections
   - have student readers take a turn reading if they so choose
4. **After the first reading,** the teacher and students may
   - discuss the story (This should always be attended to before any extension activities. This is what real readers do.)
   - reread the story as a whole group, with more students participating in the reading
   - reread the story with a partner or in small groups
   - reread with a recorded version of the story (good for individual students)
   - take a copy home to share

Some of the benefits of shared reading include:

- conveys an enjoyment of literature

- models reading/thinking process
- develops vocabulary in context of reading
- develops oral language
- makes the reading/writing connection
- enables risk-free participation
- helps participants view themselves as readers

Language Experience Stories

Language experience uses real language to illustrate the correspondence of oral to written language. Language experience bridges a child's oral language with written language through the cooperative efforts of the child dictating a story and the teacher recording what was dictated onto a chalkboard or flipchart large enough for the children to see the print. The story, once dictated, is then read aloud by the teacher and the child or children. Specific instruction in a variety of areas may then follow as determined appropriate by the teacher for that particular child or group. Such instruction can include word recognition, cueing systems (what makes sense), beginning sounds, and the meaning of punctuation.

Students find it much easier to read their own experiences written in language that sounds like them than to learn from the unfamiliar language patterns often used in published texts. It is important to record exactly what the children dictate. The children must be able to read what is stated and see that language in print, otherwise they will read what they said and not what is written on the paper. (Dictated stories may be illustrated and published and sent home for children to practice real reading with their parents.)

An example of a language experience lesson follows, based on a format in Lloyd Ollila and Margie Mayfield (1992, 156). These activities provide for active participation by each child and ample oral and written language experiences.

Language Experience Within an Activity. Language experience can add an important literacy event to an activity like making a holiday gift for parents, such as handprints in clay.

1. **Experience.** Using simple written instructions with sequenced steps, the children make their handprint gift. As instructions are given, refer to the simple instructions posted on the board. Discuss each step as it is completed, using vocabulary that includes discussion of the senses (How did it feel? Was the clay cool to touch?). Have each child mount and label the handprint with his or her name.
2. **Discussion.** When the project is completed, discuss the activity as a kind of prewriting. What did they do? Why? How do you think parents will like the gift? Why? What do you think parents might do with such a gift? As ideas are shared, write key words on the board or on chart paper.
3. **Dictation.** Have the children dictate a story about the experience. Write carefully and in print large enough for all to see. Write exactly what the

children dictate. (In a group, the teacher may use the child's name next to the sentence he dictates so the child can identify his own words.)

4. **Reading.** When the story is complete, read it out loud. The teacher reads first, but the teacher and children can do subsequent readings together. The teacher uses a pointer and runs the pointer under the text as it is being read, pointing to each word, reading in a slow, but not choppy manner. The children can take turns with the pointer as the story becomes familiar.

5. **Follow-Up.** The story can be used for several days and there are many possibilities for follow up. Some follow-up ideas include:
   - Writing sentences on sentence strips and putting them in a pocket chart. The sentences can be mixed up and put back in order.
   - Giving separate sentence strips to an individual child or pair of children, who cut the sentence into words and put the sentence back in order.
   - For early readers, writing each child's sentence on a strip and having that child match what is on the strip with what is in the story.
   - Finding repeated words and highlighting them throughout the story.
   - Identifying certain beginning sounds.
   - Typing the story and making a copy for each child. The children can then illustrate it (see Figure 4–3).
   - Continuing to reread the story over the next few weeks to reinforce and provide enjoyment and confidence.

Pair–Think–Share

The pair–think–share strategy, a thinking activity similar to the DRTA, provides opportunities for students to talk about selections being read and, in the process of thinking and talking, bring meaning to the text.

In this activity, the students work with partners. As with the DRTA, the teacher decides on stopping points for discussion and identifies these for the students. After marking these points, students read to the stopping point and then talk about what they have read. At this point most students still need some direction. The teacher can provide some ideas on the board or on a handout; for example, they might discuss the most interesting part, what was surprising, if the characters remind them of anyone they know, if they can make any personal connections, and so on. Partners are encouraged to make notes about their discussions, but not fill in worksheet answers; the students should lead the direction of the discussion. Before reading the next section, the teacher might want to give the whole group a chance to share some of the ideas arrived at in the partner discussion. The students are then ready to read the next section. The teacher's directions to pair–think–share not only communicates to students what they are expected to do, but also makes it easy for students to take responsibility for themselves. This technique is especially helpful for readers who need support as they read. It helps them work through a text and comprehend as they go along.

Suggested Procedure

1. Pair students with a partner. The teacher can decide if these should be partners of their own choosing, partners who will support each other's reading, or partners who are reading on similar developmental levels.

2. The teacher sets predetermined stopping points in the selected reading and communicates these points with the students (perhaps by writing down page numbers and paragraphs on the board or by telling the students before reading). To remind them where to stop, the students mark these stopping points lightly in their texts with a pencil or by placing small sticky notes in the text.

3. The students read to the first stopping point and then make notes about what they are thinking about at this point in the reading. These notes can be made in a log or journal, or they can be simply jotted down on the corresponding sticky note.

4. After a pair of students has finished thinking and jotting down their thoughts, they share their ideas with one other pair. They jot down any ideas that emerge from their shared discussion.

5. At this point, the teacher can ask either the entire class to share their ideas or the pairs of students can return to read the next section, repeating steps 3 and 4. The whole group can discuss their thoughts and shared ideas following the reading of the entire story.

The pair–think–share strategy has many benefits for struggling readers. The activity, which works well with both fiction and nonfiction texts, helps students feel more prepared for discussion and gives them an opportunity to construct understanding along with other students, which seems to generate more complex ideas. The activity continues to promote students taking responsibility for their own learning.

CHAPTER EIGHT

After Reading

Procedures to Support Comprehension

When proficient readers finish reading, they often look for someone to talk with about the book. This desire to continue the reading process after the reader has finished reading has led to the popularity of book clubs like Oprah's and book selections on television shows such as the *Today Show*. As teachers, we can use this natural desire to talk about reading by providing opportunities for students to do such activities in a meaningful context.

Strategies to Use After Reading

Summarizing, retelling, and connecting can help deepen comprehension, provide assessment opportunities, and most important, help readers bring closure to a pleasant and meaningful reading experience.

Summarizing/Retelling

Helping children understand how to summarize or retell takes direct instruction (discussed in detail later). Even though we can use retelling after reading as an assessment tool to check comprehension, the reader must also see purpose in such activities. Summaries written to recommend a book should be more than just school exercises; to be part of a meaningful reading experience such activities will have more purpose if shared with classmates. Retelling can be the basis for a reaction, or a part of a discussion, or a way for readers to pull together what they have just finished reading. Children can also see the difference between retelling during an assessment such as Running Record or miscue analysis and retelling as a way to share an interpretation with another reader.

Connecting

Real readers connect after reading by discussing or thinking about how the text connects to their personal experiences. Such connections can be part of discussions and literature circles (see Chapter 7) as well as response journals or reading logs (see Chapter 2). As children become more proficient readers, they begin to see that all reading connects to their lives in some way, but only if that reading is comprehended.

Story Mapping

Story mapping identifies major structural elements in a story and helps prepare students for retelling. Story maps are a type of graphic organizer that

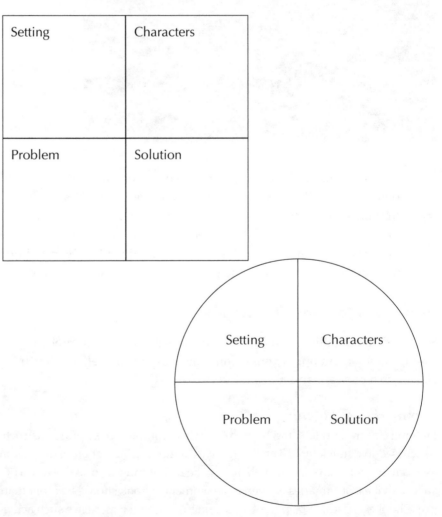

Figure 8–1 Story maps

helps readers organize and visualize the relationship of events in a story after identifying characters and setting. They also help readers see the structure of story, so they can read expecting certain types of information, in other words, predicting, based on a knowledge of how stories work and are set up.

Traditionally, the terms used for story maps reflect the terms used when discussing story grammar, terms such as *problem* and *solution*. Some primary teachers choose to use this terminology as early as first grade. If that is the case, a great deal of modeling is needed, as the terms are abstract and often difficult for children to work with. A simple map that uses the traditional terms looks some thing like that shown in Figure 8–1 (it can be set up as a circle or a block). An intermediate example is shown in Figure 8–2.

Characters	Jonas his family unit The Giver Jonas' friends
Setting	A community built on "sameness" set some time in the future.
Problem	Jonas is chosen at age 12 to be the Receiver and the Giver must pass all memories on to him.
Events leading to solution of problem	Jonas learns about the past, about pain and love. Jonas learns about release and decides the community must share memories. Jonas escapes from the community and the Giver.
Solution	Jonas reaches "elsewhere." Memories are freed.

Figure 8–2 Intermediate story map for *The Giver*

Someone-Wants-But-So

An alternative to these traditional maps is a simple type of map discussed by Kylene Beers (2003). This map accomplishes the same thing as the ones

Someone	Wants	But	So
The Three Billy Goats Gruff	to cross the bridge	The troll tries to stop them.	The big goat knocks the Troll in the water.

Figure 8–3 The "someone-wants-but-so" map for *The Three Billy Goats Gruff*

in Figure 8–2, but uses familiar vocabulary and guides the students through the mapping. With each story, the students try to complete the phrase, "Someone (who) Wants (something) But (someone else does something) So (the result)." This is illustrated in the chart in Figure 8–3.

Retelling

Retelling has been used as an assessment technique to evaluate how well a child comprehends a story; however, retelling has far more possibilities as a teaching strategy. Retelling, which is simply having the opportunity to put a story into one's own words, actually helps children to develop comprehension skills. Retelling is a flexible teaching tool that has many advantages: it requires little preparation on the part of the teacher, is appropriate for readers at all developmental levels, can involve all the language arts (reading, writing, listening, and speaking), can help readers learn about text structure and organization, and can provide a springboard for personal interaction with a story (Brown and Cambourne 1987; Glazer 1992).

Before reading a story that will be retold, readers should be encouraged to make predictions that will activate prior knowledge and help them read for a purpose, to confirm or adjust their predictions (Brown and Cambourne 1987). Retellings can be in oral or written form (including drawing), depending on the purpose a teacher decides on and the development of the reader. Retelling can be conducted in groups or individually, guided or unguided. It is important to model how to retell a story or a child might not understand what you are asking them to do. When asked to retell the story, the child might simply respond "It's about a dog" and the rest of the retelling proceeds as a question-and-answer time between reader and teacher. The aim is for students to understand what is being asked, and then feel comfortable telling the sequenced story in their own words, including all essential elements of the story. Experience with story mapping (see Figures 8–1 to 8–3) helps readers understand the parts of a story and know that including story elements such as character, setting, main event, supporting details, problem, and resolution in a logical sequence of events is what is included in a retelling.

For younger children, begin with pretelling (see Chapter 6) so that children learn the structure and procedure of thinking backward. Begin by making sure children understand how to divide stories up into things that happened in the beginning, the middle, and the end. This provides a framework of sorts to begin retelling.

Regardless of preparation, some readers still need guidance with retellings, depending on their development, their comfort with the strategy, and even their interest in the topic of the story. The goal is not to interrogate, but to guide, with questions such as "What happened next?" and "How did the story begin?"

Children can learn to self-assess as they retell by using instruments such as the one in Figure 8–4 and teachers can use retelling as an assessment tool by using instruments such as the one in Figure 8–5.

My name _____ Date _____

My friend's name _____

Title of story _____

Completed   ☐ by myself   ☐ with my friend's help

In my retelling, I remembered to include:

☐ The main character

☐ The supporting (other) characters

☐ The setting (where the story took place)

☐ The problem

☐ Important details

☐ How the story ended

☐ What I thought of the story and why

Figure 8–4 Retelling self-assessment

Student's name _____ Date _____

Title of story _____

In retelling the story, the students included:

Setting   ☐ Aided   ☐ Unaided

Main characters   ☐ Aided   ☐ Unaided

Supporting characters   ☐ Aided   ☐ Unaided

Problem   ☐ Aided   ☐ Unaided

Supporting details   ☐ Aided   ☐ Unaided

Conclusion   ☐ Aided   ☐ Unaided

Evaluation of Retelling

Understood key vocabulary

Understood cause and effect

Comments

Figure 8–5 Retelling guide

It is important to help young children understand the purposes of retelling in our lives, not just because we'll be tested on it, but also because retelling events in our lives is part of our oral language culture. In her book *Revisit, Reflect, Retell,* Linda Hoyt (1999) suggests several activities to help primary readers learn to retell.

Paper bag theatre is a simple activity that gives students a great deal of responsibility and involves children whose interests and strengths may lie in art. Children draw the setting of the story on the front of the paper bag (a forest, the three bears' house, a castle) and then draw characters and story elements to place in the bag. Children can then practice telling the story using the bag as a backdrop and using the visuals stored in the bag as props to retell. This activity can be done in small groups and used in centers or during whole-group share time.

Story bags also use simple paper bags, but instead of drawing story elements, simple props are collected in the bag and used for retelling. For example, a bowl, a dollhouse chair, and a bed can be used for "Goldilocks and Three Bears," and a red cape, a basket, cookies, a nightcap, ears, teeth, a nose, and a Woodman's cap for "Little Red Riding Hood" can be placed in the bag.

Storytelling on the overhead projector is always fun and can be used as a center activity. Students love to draw on transparencies and can draw characters and scenes from the beginning, middle, and end of the story on them. This activity not only provides a real reason for retelling, but also gives children practice with drawing as a form of writing.

Wearable art is a creative activity in which children draw characters and props they think they need to retell a story on heavy paper, cut the drawing out, and glue a small square of Velcro on the back of each piece. (Teachers must prepare a simple vest or apron made from felt for this activity.) As the children retell the story, they adhere the appropriate pieces on their apron and the audience can see the story unfold.

Line drawings are popular with children who enjoy drawing. Children can be invited to draw the story as they retell it in front of an audience. This can be done on easel paper, the chalkboard, or on transparencies. I would suggest this be presented as an option, as this activity could prove arduous for those who find drawing difficult or unpleasant.

Linguistic Roulette

Linguistic roulette, a technique developed by Jerome Hartse, can be used during literature circles or during shared reading activities (Rasinski and Padak 2000). This activity is a way to structure discussion and help students feel more confident about sharing. Linguistic roulette offers a way to make sure all students are included and have a voice in the discussion.

Suggested Procedure

1. After the class has finished reading a story or chapter of a story, each student identifies one sentence that was interesting, confusing, surprising, or special in some way.
2. Each student writes the sentence and page number from the reading on a piece of paper.
3. Once everyone has had enough time to select a sentence, each student, one at a time, reads the chosen sentence and the class as a group discusses it. I ask the student who selected the sentence to say nothing until the others in the group have discussed the sentence. After discussion is underway, the selector can then share reasons for choosing the sentence.

The linguistic roulette strategy has many benefits for both proficient and struggling readers; it encourages discussion from a variety of perspectives and it encourages students to return to the text to support their ideas, providing for a much closer reading of the text.

Response Journals

Students can use writing as a way to respond to their reading with the use of response journals. Responses should be individual but students do need support as they learn ways in which readers can respond. At the primary level, drawing is a large part of response journals, with students illustrating favorite parts and writing captions. As students get older, they begin to respond to parts of the stories and make connections to the characters and events. Students naturally respond to plot and often use response journals for a type of retelling. Teachers can model other types of responses to use in journals, such as connections, and responses to character's actions (see Figure 8–6).

Response journals can also be adapted for use as buddy journals in which two readers write back and forth to each other during the reading of a novel. The teacher might want to begin this with one group of students and use that experience as a model for illustrating the procedure to the whole class.

The most important thing to remember about response journals is that they should be a discussion or talk on paper. Students should feel free to write in their own voices, not for a grade, or to offer the correct response, but as thoughtful readers responding to the meaning brought to the text. When teachers review reading logs or response journals, they should remember response journals offer a way to get inside the head of a reader and assess how that person is reading, not to assess the writing itself. Therefore, response journals employed for this type of assessment can be replied to, but shouldn't be corrected. However, given the nature of classrooms, students want to see that their response journals are "worth something" in terms of their grade. If a grade is to be given, students could demonstrate both completeness and depth of response, depending on grade

1. Feel free to write your innermost feelings, opinions, thoughts, likes, and dislikes. This is your journal. Feel the freedom to express yourself and your personal responses to reading through it.

2. Take the time to write down anything that you are thinking while you read. The journal is a way of recording those fleeting thoughts that pass through your mind as you interact with the book. Keep your journal close by and stop to write often, whenever a thought strikes you.

3. Don't worry about the accuracy of spelling and mechanics in the journal. The content and the expression of your personal thoughts should be your primary concern. The journal will not be evaluated for a grade. Relax and share.

4. Record the page number . . . you were reading when you wrote your response. Although it may seem unimportant, you might want to look back to verify your thoughts.

5. Use one side only of your spiral notebook paper, please. Expect to read occasional, interested comments from your teacher. These comments will not be intended to judge or criticize your reactions, but will create an opportunity for use to converse about your thoughts.

6. Relate the book to your own experiences and share similar moments from your life or from books you have read in the past.

7. Ask questions while reading to help you make sense of the characters and the unraveling plot. Don't hesitate to wonder why, indicate surprise, or admit confusion. These responses often lead to an emerging understanding of the book.

8. Make predictions about what you think will happen as the plot unfolds. Validate, invalidate, or change those predictions as you proceed in the text. Don't worry about being wrong.

9. Talk to the characters as you begin to know them. Give them advice to help them. Put yourself in their place and share how you would act in a similar situation. Approve or disapprove of their values, actions, or behavior. Try to figure out what makes them react the way they do.

10. Praise or criticize the book, the author, or the literary style. Your personal tastes in literature are important and need to be shared.

11. There is no limit to the types of responses you may write. Your honesty in capturing your thoughts throughout the book is your most valuable contribution to the journal. These guidelines are meant to trigger, not limit, the kinds of things you write. Be yourself and share your personal response to literature through your journal.

Figure 8–6 Guidelines for response journals

I have included: 10 entries (2 points)

                   7 to 9 entries (1 point)

                   Fewer than 7 entries (0 points)   _____

My responses:

• were thoughtful and at least one page long (1 or 2 points)   _____

• connected to other books (1 or 2 points)   _____

• looked at issues/ideas not directly stated by author
  (inferences not just a summary) (1 or 2 points)   _____

TOTAL   _____

Grade scale: 8 points = A; 6 points = B; 4 points = C;
fewer than 3 = Incomplete/resubmit

Figure 8–7 Response journal

level. For example, with upper-elementary students, instead of reading every entry, students could identify their three best and invite an evaluation based on predetermined criteria. The grade is then clearly determined and students see that their effort "counts." A simple evaluation form, such as the one in Figure 8–7, recognizes effort and quality.

Story Frames

Story frames organize the events of a story and heighten students' awareness of story elements, which helps teach students to how to summarize.

A story frame provides a skeletal paragraph that students can fill in to prepare for discussion or writing. A story frame helps students organize events, especially young readers who have difficulty organizing the events of a story. A skeletal story frame can emphasize all or any of five areas: plot summary, setting, character analysis, character comparison, and problem. Three examples of the format, as suggested by Gerald Fowler (1982), are shown in Figure 8–8.

Semantic Webbing of Characters in a Story

Semantic webbing allows readers an opportunity to organize ideas into categories and to show the category relationships in the form of a web, which

Plot/Problem Story Frame

In this story, the problem begins when

_____

_____

After that,

_____

_____

Next,

_____

_____

The problem is finally solved when

_____

_____

Summary Story Frame

The story is about _____ who is an important character in this story.
_____ tries to _____
and _____. The story ends when
_____.

Character Analysis Story Frame

_____ is an important character in this story because
_____. Once (s)he
_____.

    In another part of the story, (s)he is _____ because
_____.

Figure 8–8 Three examples of story frames

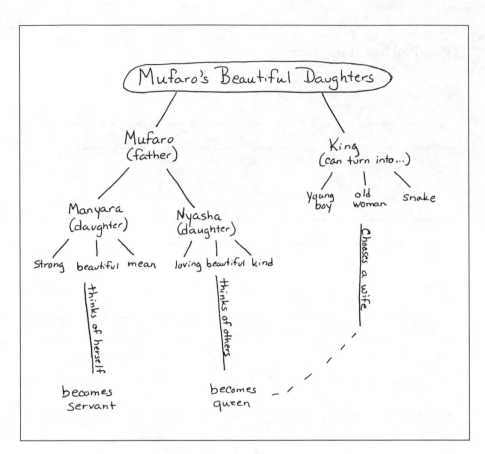

Figure 8–9 Semantic web for *Mufaro's Beautiful Daughters*

provides a visual display of understandings. Usually the teacher provides the core of the web or central question and the strands of the web are student ideas, facts, and inferences taken from the story or the reader's experiences (Freedman and Reynolds 1980).

Semantic webbing can be used before, during, and after reading. Before reading, children web possibilities or predictions, usually based on experiences. During reading, students can use information gleaned to a certain point to web possibilities or predictions of character action or plot lines. After reading, students can construct a web to demonstrate their understandings of character, story structure, and plot. For example, the connections between characters and actions can be seen in the web drawn for *Mufaro's Beautiful Daughters* (see Figure 8–9).

Seeing Stick

Another type of mapping, in which students use a visual time line or flowchart about a story or topic, is the seeing stick (Miller 1996). A seeing stick is a set of boxes, arranged vertically, that contains a sequence of events in a story or text with one picture or written discussion in each box (see Figure 8–10 and Appendix E). Visual displays, such as these, help students sequence and recall story events and can be useful to some children when retelling or discussing a story.

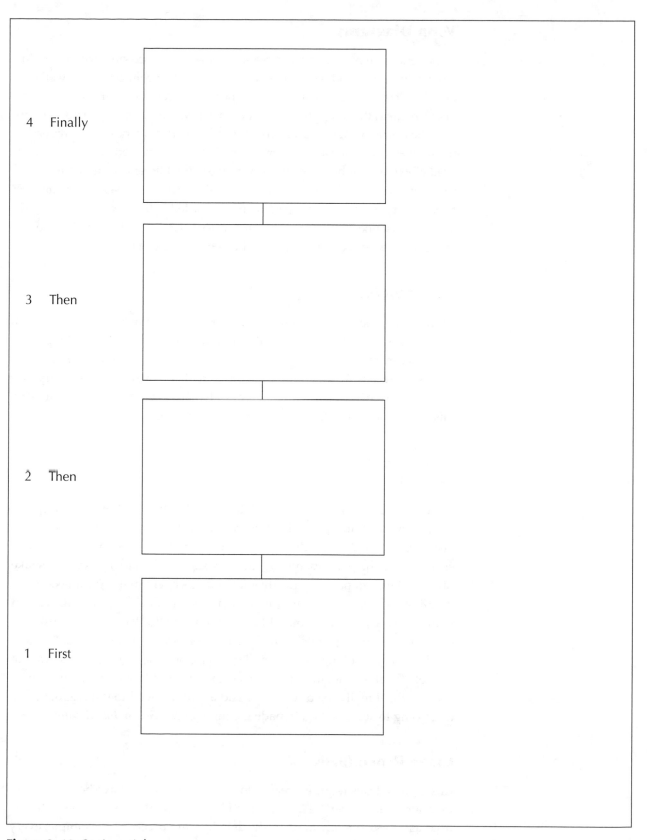

Figure 8–10 Seeing stick

Venn Diagrams

Comprehension relies in part on readers being able to see similarities and differences in stories and being able to make text-to-text connections as well as ones between text and their own life experiences. Venn diagrams are a way to organize ideas that is appropriate for both primary and intermediate students.

The teacher simply draws two circles that overlap. (Kids can do this easily themselves when they are comfortable with the activity.) Venn diagrams can be used when reading two versions of a story or two different stories with some similarities or comparing one story to a real-life incident. Ideas that are unique to each story or situation can be drawn or recorded in the area of the appropriate circle that doesn't overlap, and similarities between the two can be recorded in the middle section where the two circles overlap (see Figure 8–11).

Say Something

Conversation helps to deepen comprehension and moves students from an understanding of the text to an interpretation of it. The say something strategy can be used at all levels and can even begin with picture books. Children are simply asked to "say something" about the cover, and to move through the story constructing meaning. Teachers can help students new to this technique by modeling three types of response:

I notice . . .
I wonder why . . .
This reminds me of . . .

Each of these starters helps children build to the next level of interpretation, with the "I notice" setting the groundwork for the "I wonder why." Lea McGee (2002) of the University of Alabama takes this one step further, encouraging the participants to "catch a spark." When real discussions take place in the classroom, sparks fly and students begin making connections, building on each other's interpretation and ideas. Such opportunities begin with, "I really like what you said and it made me think of . . . ." For example, when discussing *Hatchet* by Gary Paulsen, someone might say, "He needs to begin looking for food and deciding how he's going to take care of himself." A classmate might "catch a spark" from this statement and continue with, "I really liked what you said about his need to think about how he's going to survive, and it made me think of *My Side of the Mountain*."

Cloze Procedures

Cloze procedures require a reader to supply words that have been deleted from a passage; it can be used for both assessment and instruction. When used as an assessment strategy, the deletions are precise; for example, every fifth or seventh word would be deleted, and the reader would be asked to supply the word or choose from selections to fill in the blank.

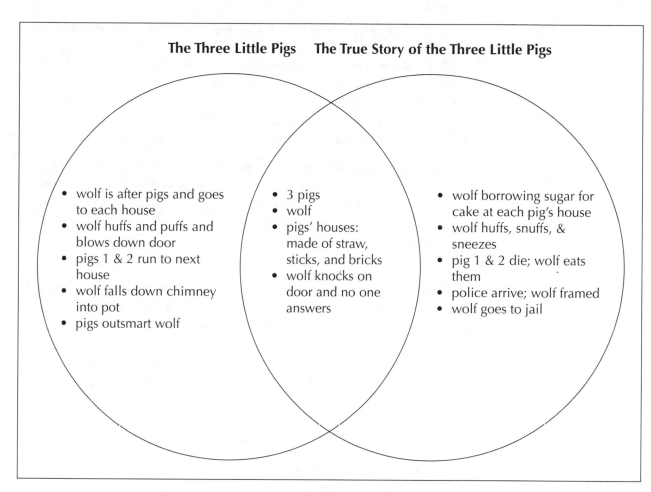

The Three Little Pigs   The True Story of the Three Little Pigs

- wolf is after pigs and goes to each house
- wolf huffs and puffs and blows down door
- pigs 1 & 2 run to next house
- wolf falls down chimney into pot
- pigs outsmart wolf

- 3 pigs
- wolf
- pigs' houses: made of straw, sticks, and bricks
- wolf knocks on door and no one answers

- wolf borrowing sugar for cake at each pig's house
- wolf huffs, snuffs, & sneezes
- pig 1 & 2 die; wolf eats them
- police arrive; wolf framed
- wolf goes to jail

Figure 8–11   Venn diagram of *The Three Little Pigs* and *The True Story of the Three Little Pigs*

Cloze procedures, however, can also be used for instructional purposes. In this case, instead of every fifth or seventh word being deleted, the teacher deletes words that require the reader to use strategies that focus on meaning (semantic cues), structure of the language (syntactic cues), or visual cues (graphic cues). In the case of meaning or structure cues, whole words are deleted, but in the case of visual cues, the deletions are partial, such as only the beginning sound being provided. The objective is not word-perfect reading, but meaning making. Any response that makes sense is acceptable, but with visual cues the possibilities are more limited because part of the word is provided.

Teachers might model cloze procedures as a type of think-aloud (see Chapter 7) during shared reading by using a Big Book that has words that the teacher has chosen before the reading session to cover with Post-it notes or tape. As the teacher reads aloud and comes to a covered-up word, she models how she tries to decide what would be an appropriate word to fit in the covered word space. She will emphasize a "what makes sense" approach as she uses the meaning of the surrounding words, its place in the sentence, and sometimes skipping over it and reading to the end of the sentence. Such modeling can also be done with students of all ages using transparencies with selections of books on the transparency with blanks for certain words. It is best to use paragraphs rather than individual sentences so that students can see the meaning of the story grow and can use cues from the making of meaning in the selection. Don Holdaway (1980), in *Independence in Reading*, offers suggestions for many different ways to use cloze activities (78).

1. **Reading aloud.** With even the youngest readers, inviting children to supply words left out as you read along invites them to make sense from text. Children also learn to supply rhyming words when reading patterned stories that can help with both phonemic awareness and meaning making. Asking children, "How did you know that was the word?" often invites the children to respond with such answers as "because it makes sense."

2. **Riddles.** Again, such an activity can begin with very young children and encourages them to use prediction, justification, and meaning making. An example: What am I? I am often red and children ride in me. (Children make predictions and then the teacher continues.) I have four wheels and someone pulls me. (Predictions are narrowed and clues are continued, if needed.) I can sometimes hold two children and sometimes a parent pulls me on the sidewalk with the children inside me. (A wagon.) Riddles can also be written first by the teacher, and as the children become more familiar with the format, by the students themselves.

3. **Riddle cloze.** After playing with riddles, it is easy for children to move to riddles written with the cloze technique.

> I'm red and have four wheels. You can _____ in me. When you are
> s_____-ing in me, someone _____ me down the sidewalk. I am
> a wagon.

4. **Nursery rhyme cloze.** This is an easy way to introduce children to cloze if they are familiar with nursery rhymes.

> Jack and Jill went up the _____ to fetch a pail of _____. Jack fell
> _____ and broke his crown, and _____ came tumbling after.

5. **Language experience cloze.** Children love to play with the stories they create, and such stories are usually quite predictable. Stories written during language experience can be turned into cloze passages, which children love to read and fill in the blanks (see Chapter 7).

6. **Poetry Cloze.** Children must think of rhyme, rhythm, and language as they think of words deleted from a poem. This works well with older children as well as younger ones depending on the complexity of the poem.

7. **"Scratch it" cloze.** After preparing a passage with permanent marker on an overhead transparency, cover key words with white out. When children guess what the word should be, they use a coin to scratch off the white covering. This same strategy can be used with masking tape or colored tape.

8. **Rebus cloze.** For younger or beginning readers, a picture clue can be used in place of a word. For example:

I love you

I love singing

Interpretive Questions

During literature circle conversations or in small group or whole class *grand conversations* (Eeds and Wells 1989), teacher questioning can make or break a conversation. Rather than comprehension questions (we all know what those are), teachers can try interpretive questions. These questions allow children to consider more than one meaning of a story or more than one perspective of a character or the character's actions. It can also allow readers to consider multiple interpretations of a story outcome or event. Such questions are used to stimulate conversation, not to direct it. For example, after reading *Shiloh*, the teacher might ask, "Why do you think he lied to his dad? How do you think he felt? Why do you think he finally gave him the dog?" And after reading *The Paper Bag Princess* by Robert Munsch, the teacher might ask, "What kind of person is the Princess? Why wouldn't she marry Ronald?"

Write and Share[2]

Proficient readers know that making meaning when responding to literature is more in-depth and interesting when sharing with other readers. Write and Share[2], a comprehension strategy developed by Jane Davidson (1987), gives readers a chance to make meaning with others as they write twice and share twice in response to text they have read.

As with literature circles (see Chapter 7), students are grouped in clusters of three to five, all reading the same text. After reading, students jot down ideas or phrases that have come to their minds while reading. In this case, sentence and organization are not necessary, just the recording of ideas. This first write is followed by a discussion in which the notes are used for the sharing of ideas and reactions to the reading. When the group is finished with the first share, the students write again, this time developing thoughts, ideas, connections, and so on into prose, using their first brief notes, discussions, ideas, and the text itself. After the writing, students again share, this time discussing their written piece and the text. Sometimes a volunteer from each group reads a written response to the entire class, helping to share group responses with all the other groups, providing opportunity for even more meaning making.

Compare and Contrast Charts

Proficient readers naturally compare and contrast reading as a part of their interaction with various texts. In classrooms, we want to provide opportunities for our students to do this in ways that are natural outgrowths of their reading experiences (They'll also be expected to do this on many state and national reading tests.)

Rasinski and Padak (2000) suggest the use of what they call compare and contrast charts. Using a typical grid, a list is made of the texts that are to be compared or contrasted (see Figure 8–12). These can include various types of books (fantasy, historical fiction, picture books), authors (Katherine Paterson, Tomie DePaola), or characters in a particular book or series (*Little House on the Prairie, American Girl, Junie B. Jones*). On the other side of the grid, the students record key characteristics that distinguish one item from another. These grids can be completed individually, in pairs, or by groups, and they can be used by students at any grade level, from first grade to eighth grade.

Artful Artist or Sketch to Stretch

Teachers have long been aware of the power of drawing in aiding comprehension. The artful artist or sketch to stretch technique has a reader draw or sketch a favorite scene, memorable event, or character's actions from a recent reading. Encourage students to experiment and assure them that there are many ways to represent personal meaning. The artist then shows the sketch to a small group of students who have also read the same text. The group then responds to the drawing, with the artist at first saying nothing, touching upon points such as

Compare and Contrast Books by Kevin Henkes

Title	Main Characters (how they are special)	Lesson (important idea)	Our Feelings
Chester's Way	Chester and Wilson—like same things Lilly—tries new things	New kids can be fun to know.	It's funny like in real life.
Chrysanthemum	Chrysanthemum—unususal name Mrs. Twinkle—teacher whose name is Delphinium	Everyone's name is cool; unusual names are interesting.	Funny but happy for Chrysanthemum in the end.
Sheila Rae's Peppermint Stick	Sheila Rae—had peppermint stick Louise—wanted some	It's nice to share.	Glad Louise gets some peppermint stick.
Lilly's Purple Plastic Purse	Lilly—wants to be a teacher someday Mr. Slinger—a wonder teacher	We shouldn't be mean when we are angry; we should apologize when we're wrong.	We know Lilly felt bad; Mr. Slinger makes us feel safe and happy.

Figure 8–12 Example of a compare and contrast chart

Figure 8–13 Artful artist's rendering of a birthday cake and eleven smaller figures of a girl

- Why they think the artist found this important.
- How they think the artist felt about this scene.
- What they think the artist saw happening here.
- Whether they connected to this in the way the artist did as a reader.

Students build on the ideas and reactions of others and eventually the artist joins the conversation by sharing her ideas and feelings.

Based on the Harvey Daniels' (2002) *artful artist* role in literature circles and Jerome Harste's *sketch to stretch* activity (Short, Harste, and Burke 1996), the technique works for students of all ages. The artistic ability of the responder is not important; the opportunity to stimulate thought and discussion with the aid of a nonverbal prompt is.

For example, after reading the short story "Eleven" by Sandra Cisneros, a reader responded with the drawing shown in Figure 8–13. The discussion that followed went something like this:

- "This is how the girl felt on her eleventh birthday. It was ruined when the teacher embarrassed her. She felt terrible and not at all like an eleven year old."
- "She felt some of the feeling you feel when you're three. She wanted to cry and probably disappear."
- "She felt like she was ten and nine and eight and seven and six and five and four and three and two and one year old. She's really all these ages combined now that she's eleven."
- "I connected to this especially because I just had my tenth birthday. People kept asking me if I felt different being double digits but I didn't really feel any different from how I felt last week."

Strategies Good Readers Use

During lessons in which teaching comprehension is an objective, the following are processes that can be modeled, discussed, and supported (Goodman, Watson, and Burke 1996; Pearson, Roehler, Dole, and Duffy 1992; Pressley et al. 2001; Weaver 2002).

- **Activating prior knowledge**—helping students "get ready to read" by looking at the title, cover of the book, and so on, and making initial predictions with techniques such as experience-text-relationships (ETR) (Au 1993) and KWL charts.

- **Predicting**—a part of proficient reading that can be directly taught through techniques such as DRTA (see Chapter 7).
- **Generating visual images**—graphic organizers such as webs, maps, trees, diagrams, charts, and so on that provide a visual representation of the text and relationships within the text (see Chapters 4 and 6).
- **Summarizing**—helping students understand the main points and supporting details can be accomplished in literature logs, during literature circles, or through graphic organizers.
- **Self-questioning**—showing readers that we read to answer our own questions and we adjust those questions as we gather more information and understanding; think-alouds are examples of teaching strategies that employ self-questioning (see Chapter 7).
- **Analyzing text for story grammar elements**—understanding how stories are organized to include character, setting, and so on. Story maps help students understand such organization.
- **Inferencing**—helping students to use what is implied to bring meaning to text can be accomplished during reading through reciprocal teaching, DRTA, and comprehensive strategy lessons and during discussion following reading.
- **Distinguishing important information**—connects to reader response, in that students judge information as important based on their own experience. However, using text to support interpretations to help students distinguish what is important can be taught through discussion during literature circles and when using response journals.
- **Synthesizing**—putting the pieces together and seeing connections through literature circles, mapping, and summarizing.
- **Monitoring**—checking predictions, adjusting and confirming as necessary.
- **Learning to repair faulty comprehension**—remembering that reading is making sense is strengthened by discussion, rereading, and writing.

It's important for teachers to guide students through the process of strategic reading before, during, and after reading a selection. An example of the types of questions teachers can ask is shown in Figure 8–14. A checklist that students can use to monitor their reading to see what strategies they use regularly and to remind them of some they may be overlooking is shown in Figure 8–15.

Questions Teachers Can Ask *Before* Children Read

1. What can you tell from the title of this book? What do you think it might be about?

2. What does the cover illustration tell you about what this book will be about?

3. What do you already know about _____ (topic)?

4. What are some things you might learn or find out about in this story?

5. Why do you think the author wrote about this?

6. What kind of questions do you want to ask yourself before you begin reading this?

7. Where do you think this story takes place? What tells you that?

8. Do you have any ideas about any of the characters?

Questions Teachers Can Ask *While* Children Read

1. What do you think will happen next?

2. Were your predictions correct? Did you want to adjust any predictions?

3. Does the story make sense so far?

4. What has happened so far?

5. What is interesting so far?

6. Can you see what is happening in your mind?

7. What are you doing when you come to words you don't know?

8. What parts are difficult to understand? How are you working at understanding them?

Questions Teachers Can Ask *After* Children Read

1. What are the answers to the questions you asked during my reading?

2. What did you think of this story? What did you learn?

3. Did you like the story? Why or why not?

4. Did the story end the way you thought it would? Did you like the ending? Where could it go from here?

5. How would you summarize this story? How would you describe it to someone who may want to read it?

6. Are there any parts you want to read again either to deepen your understanding or because you want to talk about it?

7. How did this story connect to your life?

8. Did this story remind you of any others you have read?

Figure 8–14 Questions to help children become strategic readers

Name _____ Date _____

Story title _____

When we read, we use strategies before, during, and after reading. Check the ones you used in this reading.

Before Reading

☐ I looked at the cover, title, author, and thought about what this book/story was going to be about.

☐ I read the back of the book or the book jacket to get more information about the book.

☐ I asked myself questions about what I was about to read.

☐ I predicted what this book/story was going to be about.

☐ I thought about how this book/story connected to what I already know.

☐ I looked through the book, doing a picture walk or looking at heading or graphs.

During Reading

☐ I see what is happening in my mind.

☐ I make predictions as I read.

☐ I stop and ask myself questions to see if I understand what I am reading.

☐ I reread confusing parts.

☐ I used context clues to understand new words, or I skipped them and read ahead.

☐ I slowed down when I started getting confused.

☐ I kept reading when I was confused to see if I could get clues and then I reread.

☐ I asked questions when I needed help understanding (to myself, a fellow reader, or the teacher).

After Reading

☐ I retell or summarize.

☐ I connect what I read to my own life.

☐ I reread to clear up questions or enjoy parts I liked.

☐ I draw, write, or talk about what I've read and my reactions to the story.

☐ I think about where the story might go from here or if I want to read another book about this topic or by the same author.

Figure 8–15 A checklist of reading strategies

The thirty-seven most useful phonograms, or *word families*, are found in hundreds of words children read and write (Wylie and Durrell 1970).

ack	at	ight	op
ail	ate	ill	ore
ain	aw	in	ot
ake	ay	ine	uck
ale	eat	ing	ug
ame	ell	ink	ump
ar	est	ip	unk
ank	ice	it	
ap	ick	ock	
ash	ide	oke	

Making a Children's Book/Collection of Writing

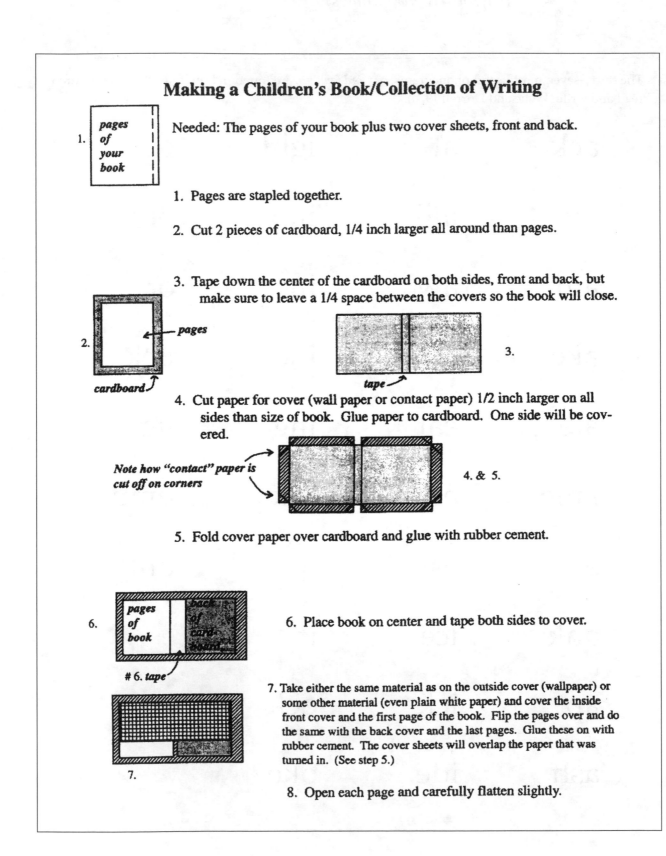

Needed: The pages of your book plus two cover sheets, front and back.

1. Pages are stapled together.

2. Cut 2 pieces of cardboard, 1/4 inch larger all around than pages.

3. Tape down the center of the cardboard on both sides, front and back, but make sure to leave a 1/4 space between the covers so the book will close.

4. Cut paper for cover (wall paper or contact paper) 1/2 inch larger on all sides than size of book. Glue paper to cardboard. One side will be covered.

5. Fold cover paper over cardboard and glue with rubber cement.

6. Place book on center and tape both sides to cover.

7. Take either the same material as on the outside cover (wallpaper) or some other material (even plain white paper) and cover the inside front cover and the first page of the book. Flip the pages over and do the same with the back cover and the last pages. Glue these on with rubber cement. The cover sheets will overlap the paper that was turned in. (See step 5.)

8. Open each page and carefully flatten slightly.

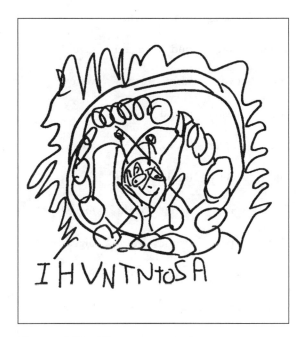

Phonemic Spelling

Letter name spelling; ". . . I would fly away and get stuck in a tree"

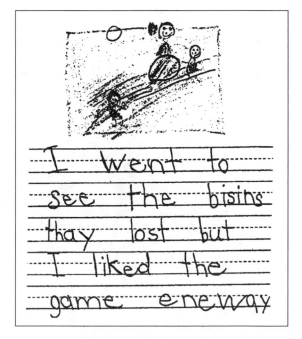

Transitional Spelling

Phonemic Spelling

APPENDIX D *Bag Words*

man	gave	us	after	that	how	be	made	does	brown	with	ate
know	once	did	than	upon	fly	now	found	from	find	again	give
about	had	what	there	help	has	long	him	over	want	her	were
his	live	any	if	got	tell	its	they	wish	round	went	or
many	could	soon	walk	say	ten	them	ask	under	let	our	always
would	not	put	take	your	out	but	seven	pretty	think	clean	because
drink	warm	kind	show	four	must	shall	laugh	grow	done	eight	myself
very	hurt	why	small	better	hold	which	five	open	read	yes	together
these	best	every	write	where	just	for	use	sit	white	fall	their
sleep	today	goes	both	keep	bring	sing	own	pull	cut	well	before
those	six	wash	full	draw	much	only	start	please	right	hot	work
thank	off	seen	light	pick	never	and	at	all	am	are	around
away	big	can	black	blue	come	but	down	funny	by	for	go
call	he	good	do	is	green	sat	jump	have	fast	here	like
get	little	me	going	look	into	my	it	make	not	of	not
on	play	old	one	red	out	ran	run	was	saw	said	who
too	see	she	three	the	some	we	this	stop	will	to	yellow

Story Summarizer

Your job is to summarize what the story was about. You may use the seeing stick to record the key points or events of the story.

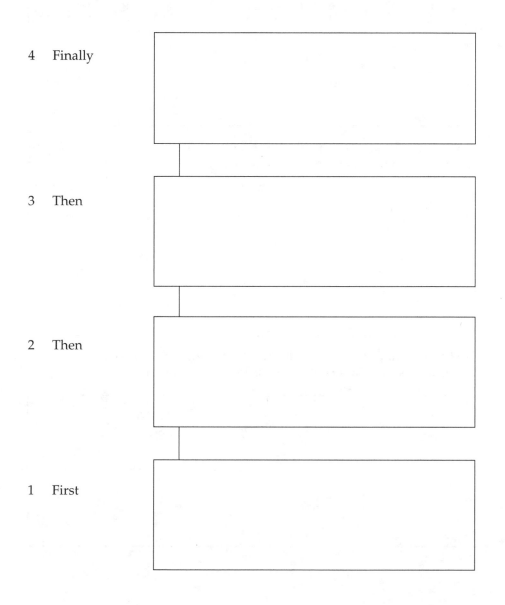

4 Finally

3 Then

2 Then

1 First

Connection Finder

Your job is to connect a part of the story to your life. Try to make text-to-text, text-to-world, or text-to-self connections.

Text-to-text. Have you ever read a similar story or seen a TV show or movie that reminds you of this story? Explain how they are similar.

Text-to-self. Has something like this ever happened to you or someone you know? How did you feel or react in that situation?

Text-to-world. Have you ever heard of anything like this before? How did you learn about it (in school, someone told you, after school . . .)?

Discussion Leader

Your job is to help your group think about this story. Think of things you'd like the group to talk about. You may use the question starters below to write the questions to lead the discussion in your group.

I wonder why . . . ?

Did you ever . . . ?

What did you think of . . . ?

What was your favorite part?

I thought it was interesting that/when . . . ; what did you think?

Word Keeper

What words in the story were new, interesting, confusing, or important to you? Write the word in the correct alphabet box and the page number where you found it in the story. Be ready to discuss what words you chose and why you chose them when we look at these words from our story together.

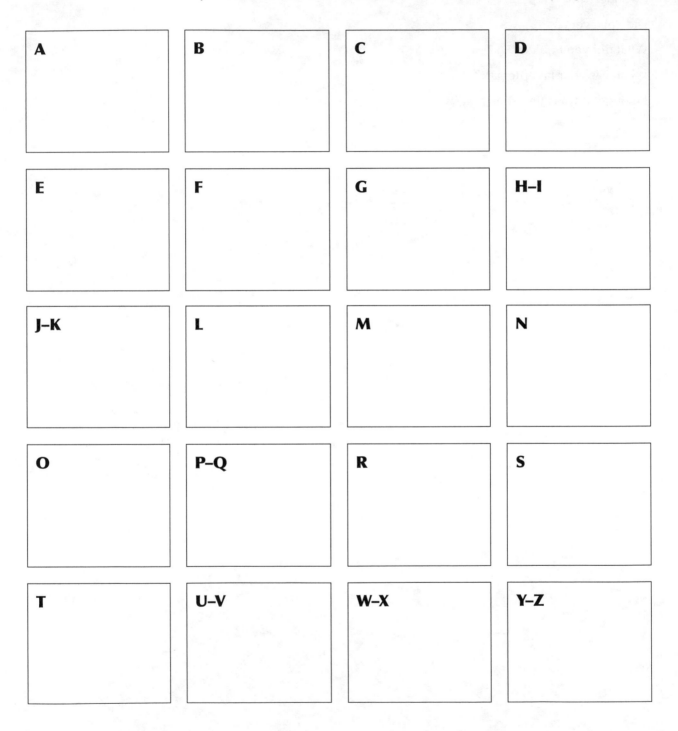

A	B	C	D
E	F	G	H–I
J–K	L	M	N
O	P–Q	R	S
T	U–V	W–X	Y–Z

Artist

Choose a part of the story you liked or thought was important. Draw a picture of it. The group will then try to guess which part of the story you chose and why you thought it was important in the story. Be prepared to discuss your drawing, why you drew it, and why that part of the story was interesting or important to you.

Passage Finder

Look through the story again. Find a particular passage in the story that you enjoyed or thought was significant. It could be a passage that was funny, interesting, confusing, or important in some way. You may mark the place with a Post-It note. Be prepared to discuss your passage with the group. Record the page number and the first few (four or five) words to help you locate the passage:

Page number _____

Begins with . . .

My reason(s) for choosing this passage:

Children's Literature Cited

Bat Loves the Night. Nicola Davies. New York: Scholastic, 2001.

Brown Bear, Brown Bear. Bill Martin, Jr. New York: Holt, 1983.

Cat in the Hat, The. Dr. Seuss. New York: Beginner Books, 1957.

Cay, The. Theodore Taylor. Garden City, NY: Doubleday, 1969.

Chester's Way. Kevin Henkes. Orlando, FL: Harcourt Brace Jovanovich, 1988.

Chick A Chick A Boom Boom. Bill Martin Jr. and John Archambault. New York: Simon & Schuster, 1989.

Chicken Soup with Rice. Maurice Sendak. New York: Scholastic, 1981.

Chrysanthemum. Kevin Henkes. New York: Greenwillow, 1991.

Doorbell Rang, The. Pat Hutchins. New York: Greenwillow, 1986.

Eating the Alphabet: Fruits and Vegetables from A to Z. Lois Ehlert. New York: Scholastic, 1989.

"Eleven" in *Woman Hollering Creek*. Sandra Cisneros. New York: Random House, 1991.

Fat Cat, The. Jack Kent. New York: Scholastic, 1971.

Five Little Monkeys. E. Christelow. New York: Clarion, 1989.

Gathering Blue. Lois Lowry. Boston: Houghton Mifflin, 2000.

Giver, The. Lois Lowry. New York: Bantam Doubleday, 1993.

Goodnight Moon. Margaret Wise Brown. New York: Harper & Row, 1947.

Grouchy Ladybug, The. Eric Carle. New York: Crowell, 1977.

Hatchet. Gary Paulsen. New York: Dell, 1987.

Hattie and the Fox. Mem Fox. New York: Bradbury, 1992.

Hush Little Baby (alternate version). Margot Zemach. New York: Dutton, 1976.

I Know an Old Lady Who Swallowed a Fly. Nadine Wescott. Boston: Houghton Mifflin, 1980.

I Went Walking. Sue Williams. Orlando, FL: Harcourt Brace, 1992.

If You Give a Mouse a Cookie. Laura Joffe Numeroff. New York: Harper & Row, 1985.

If You Take a Mouse to the Movies. Laura Joffe Numeroff. New York: Scholastic, 2000.

Is Your Mama a Llama? Deborah Guarino. New York: Scholastic, 1989.

Jake Baked a Cake. B. G. Hennessy. New York: Viking, 1990.

Jesse Bear, What Will You Wear? N. W. Cakstrom. New York: Scholastic, 1986.

Jigaree, The. Joy Cowley. Bothell, WA: Wright Group, 1987.

Light in the Attic, A. Shel Silverstein. New York: HarperCollins, 1981.

Little Red Hen, The. Paul Galdone. New York: Scholastic, 1973.

Lilly's Purple Plastic Purse. Kevin Henkes. New York: Greenwillow, 1996.

Make a Joyful Noise: A Poem in Two Voices. Paul Fleischman. New York: HarperCollins, 1988.

Mary Wore Her Red Dress. Merle Peek. New York: Clarion, 1985.

Miss Nelson Is Missing. H. Allard and J. Marshall. Boston: Houghton Mifflin, 1977.

Mrs. Wishy-Washy. Joy Cowley. Bothell, WA: Wright Group, 1987.

Mufaro's Beautiful Daughters. J. Steptoe. New York: Lothrop, Lee & Shepard, 1987.

My Side of the Mountain. Jean Craighead George. New York: Puffin Books, 1988.

Number the Stars. Lois Lowry. New York: Bantam Doubleday, 1989.

Outsiders, The. S. E. Hinton. Boston: G. K. Hall, 1989.

Over the Meadow. Ezra Jack Keats. New York: Scholastic, 1971.

Owl Moon. Jane Yolen. New York: Philomel, 1987.

Paper Bag Princess, The. Robert N. Munsch. Toronto: Annick Press, 1980.

Polar Bear, Polar Bear. Bill Martin Jr. New York: Holt, 1991.

Rosie's Walk. Pat Hutchins. New York: MacMillan, 1968.

Seven Little Rabbits. John Becker. New York: Scholastic, 1973.

Sheep in a Jeep. Nancy Shaw. Boston: Houghton Mifflin, 1989.

Sheila Rae's Peppermint Stick. Kevin Henkes. New York: Greenwillow, 1993.

Shiloh. Phyllis Reynolds Naylor. New York: Bantam Doubleday, 1991.

Something from Nothing. Phoebe Gilman. New York: Scholastic, 1992.

There's a Wocket in My Pocket. Dr. Seuss. New York: Random House, 1974.

This Old Man. Pam Adams. New York: Grosset & Dunlop, 1974.

Thump, Thump, Rat-a-tat-tat. Gene Baer. New York: Harper & Row, 1989.

Toby's Alphabet Walk. Cyndy Szekeres. New York: Little Simon, 2000.

True Story of the Three Little Pigs, The. Jan Scieszka. New York: Scholastic, 1991.

Turtle Time. Sandol Stoddard. New York: Houghton Mifflin, 1995.

Very Busy Spider, The. Eric Carle. New York: Philomel, 1985.

Very Hungry Caterpillar, The. Eric Carle. New York: Philomel, 1969.

We're Going on a Bear Hunt. Michael Rosen. New York: Margaret K. McElderry Books, 1989.

Wheels on the Bus, The. Maryann Kovakski. New York: Little Brown, 1987.

Who Is Coming? Patricia McKissack. Chicago: Children's Press, 1986.

Whose Mouse Are You? Robert Kraus. New York: Macmillan, 1970.

Works Cited

Au, K. H. 1993. *Literacy Instruction in Multicultural Settings.* New York: Harcourt Brace Jovanovich.

Beers, K. 2003. *When Kids Can't Read, What Teachers Can Do: A Guide for Teachers 6–12.* Portsmouth, NH: Heinemann.

Benson, V., and C. Cummins. 2000. *The Power of Retelling: Developmental Steps for Building Comprehension.* Bothell, WA: Wright Group.

Brown, H., and B. Cambourne. 1987. *Read and Retell.* Portsmouth, NH: Heinemann.

Clay, M. M. 1995. *Reading Recovery: A Guidebook for Teachers.* Portsmouth, NH: Heinemann.

———. 2000. *Running Records for Classroom Teachers.* Portsmouth, NH: Heinemann.

Copenhaver, J. 2001. "Running Out of Time: Rushed Read-alouds in a Primary Classroom." *Language Arts* 79 (2): 148–59.

Cramer, R. L. 1975. "Reading to Children: Why and How." *The Reading Teacher* 28 (5): 460–63.

Cunningham, P. M., and J. W. Cunningham. 1992. "'Making Words': Enhancing the Invented Spelling Decoding Connection." *The Reading Teacher* 46 (October): 106–15.

Cunningham, P. M., and D. Hall. 1998. *Month-by-Month Phonics for Third Grade.* Greenboro, NC: Carson Dellosa.

Cunningham, P., D. Hall, and C. Sigmon. 1999. *The Teacher's Guide to the Four Blocks.* Greensboro, NC: Carson Dellosa.

Daniels, H. 2002. *Literature Circles: Voice and Choice in Book Clubs and Reading Groups,* 2d ed. Portland, ME: Stenhouse.

Daniels, H., and N. Steineke. 2004. *Mini-Lessons for Literature Circles.* Portsmouth, NH: Heinemann.

Davidson, J. 1987. "Writing Across the Curriculum." Paper presented at the meeting of the Language Experience Special Interest Council, DeKalb, IL, June.

Dowhower, S. 1999. "Supporting a Strategic Stance in the Class: A Comprehensive Framework for Helping Teachers Help Students to Be Strategic." *The Reading Teacher* 52 (6): 672–88.

Durrell, D. D. 1958. "Success in First-Grade Reading." *Journal of Education* 148: 1–8.

Eeds, M., and D. Wells. 1989. "Grand Conversations: An Exploration of Meaning Construction in Literature Study Groups." *Research in the Teaching of English* 23 (1): 4–29.

Elkonin, D. B. 1973. "Reading in the USSR." In *Comparative Reading*, ed. J. Downing, 551–79. New York: Macmillan.

Five, C. L., and M. Dionisio. 1999. "Setting Up the Environment for Success." *School Talk* 4 (2): 1–4.

Fountas, I., and G. S. Pinnell. 1996. *Guided Reading: Good First Teaching for All Children*. Portsmouth, NH: Heinemann.

Fowler, G. L. 1982. "Developing Comprehension Skills in Primary Students Through the Use of Story Frames." *The Reading Teacher* 36: 176–79.

Freedman, G., and E. G. Reynolds. 1980. "Enriching Basal Reader Lessons with Semantic Webbing." *The Reading Teacher* 33 (6): 677–84.

Glazer, S. M. 1992. "Assessment in Classrooms: Reality and Fantasy." *Teaching PreK–8* 22 (May): 62–4.

Glazer, S. M., and C. Brown. 1993. *Portfolios and Beyond: Collaborative Assessment in Reading and Writing*. Norwood, MA: Christopher-Gordon.

Goodman, K. 1991. "Revaluing Readers and Reading." In *With Promise: Redefining Reading and Writing for "Special" Students*, ed. S. Stires, 127–35. Portsmouth, NH: Heinemann.

———. 1994. "Reading, Writing, and Written Texts: A Transactional Psycholinguistic View." In *Theoretical Models and Processes of Reading*, 4th ed., ed. R. B. Ruddell, M. R. Ruddell, and H. Singer, 1093–130. Newark, DE: International Reading Association.

Goodman, Y. M. 1992. "Bookhandling Knowledge Test." In *Whole Language Catalogue Supplement on Authentic Assessment*, ed. K. Goodman, L. Bridges Bird, and Y. Goodman. Santa Rosa, CA: American School Publishers.

Goodman, Y. M., and C. L. Burke. 1972. *Reading Miscue Inventory Manual: Procedures for Diagnosis and Evaluation*. New York: Macmillan.

Goodman, Y. M., D. J. Watson, and C. L. Burke. 1996. *Reading Miscue Inventory: Alternative Procedures*, 2d ed. Katonah, NY: Richard C. Owen.

Gray, W. S. 1946. *On Their Own in Reading*. Chicago: Scott, Foresman.

Hancock, M. R. 1993. "Exploring and Extending Personal Responses Through Literature Journals." *The Reading Teacher* 46 (October): 466–74.

———. 2000. *A Celebration of Literature and Response*. Upper Saddle River, NJ: Merrill.

Hansen, J. 1981. "The Effects of Inference Training and Practice on Young Children's Reading Comprehension." *Reading Research Quarterly* 16: 321–417.

Harp, B. 1989. "When the Principal Asks: 'Why Aren't You Using the Phonics Workbooks?'" *The Reading Teacher* 42 (January): 326–27.

Harste, J., V. Woodward, and C. Burke. 1984. *Language Stories and Literacy Lessons.* Portsmouth, NH: Heinemann.

Hill, B. C., N. Johnson, and K. S. Noe. 1995. *Literature Circles and Response.* Norwood, MA: Christopher-Gordon.

Hill, B. C., C. Rubtic, and L. Norwick. 1998. *Classroom Based Assessment.* Norwood, MA: Christopher-Gordon.

Hill, B. C., K. S. Noe, and N. Johnson. 2001. *Literature Circles Resource Guide.* Norwood, MA: Christopher-Gordon.

Hinson, B., ed. 2000. *New Directions in Reading Instruction: Revised Edition.* Newark, DE: International Reading Association.

Holdaway, D. 1980. *Independence in Reading,* 2d ed. Sydney: Ashton-Scholastic.

Hoyt, L. 1999. *Revisit, Reflect, Retell: Strategies for Improving Reading Comprehension.* Portsmouth, NH: Heinemann.

Manzo, A. V. 1969. "The ReQuest Procedure." *Journal of Reading* 11: 123–26.

Martens, P. 1998. "Using Retrospective Miscue Analysis to Inquire: Learning from Michael." *The Reading Teacher* 52 (October): 176–80.

McGee, L. 2002. "Catch a Spark." Presentation at the annual meeting of Keystone Reading Association Conference, Seven Springs, PA, October.

Miller, E. 1996. "The Seeing Sticks." *Journal of Adolescent and Adult Literacy* 39 (April): 584–85.

Moore, R., and C. Gilles. 2005. *Reading Conversations: Retrospective Miscue Analysis with Struggling Readers, Grades 4–12.* Portsmouth, NH: Heinemann.

Morrow, L. M. 1989. "Designing the Classroom to Promote Literacy Development." In *Emerging Literacy: Young Children Learn to Read and Write,* eds. D. S. Strickland and L. M. Morrow. Newark, DE: International Reading Association.

Noe, K. S., and N. Johnson. 1999. *Getting Started with Literature Circles.* Norwood, MA: Christopher-Gordon.

Ohnmact, D. C. 1969. "The Effects of Letter Knowledge on Achievement in Reading in the First Grade." Presentation at the annual meeting of American Education Research Association, Los Angeles, CA, April.

Ollila, L., and M. Mayfield, eds. 1992. *Emerging Literacy: Preschool, Kindergarten, and Primary Grades.* Needham Heights, MA: Allyn and Bacon.

Owocki, G. 2003. *Comprehension: Strategic Instruction for K–3 Students.* Portsmouth, NH: Heinemann.

Palincsar, A., and A. L. Brown. 1984. "Reciprocal Teaching of Comprehension-Fostering and Comprehension-Monitoring Activities." *Cognition and Instruction* 1: 117–75.

Pearson, P. D., L. R. Roehler, J. A. Dole, and G. G. Duffy. 1992. "Developing Expertise in Reading Comprehension." In *What Research Has to Say*

About Reading Instruction, eds. S. J. Samuels and A. E. Farstrup, 145–99. Newark, DE: International Reading Association.

Pinnell, G. S., and I. Fountas. 2004. *Sing a Song of Poetry* series, K–2. Portsmouth, NH: Heinemann/FirstHand.

Pressley, M., R. L. Allington, R. Wharton-McDonald, C. C. Block, and L. M. Morrow. 2001. *Learning to Read: Lessons from Exemplary First-Grade Classrooms*. New York: Guilford.

Rasinski, T., and N. Padak. 2000. *Effective Reading Strategies: Teaching Children Who Find Reading Difficult*, 2d ed. New York: Prentice-Hall.

Ruddell, M. R. 1993. *Teaching Context Reading and Writing*. Boston: Allyn & Bacon.

Samuels, S. J. 1972. "The Effect of Letter-Name Knowledge on Learning to Read." *American Educational Research Journal* 1: 65–74.

———. 1979. "The Method of Repeated Readings." *The Reading Teacher* 32: 403–8.

Short, K., J. Harste, and C. Burke. 1996. *Creating Classrooms for Authors and Inquirers*, 2d ed. Portsmouth, NH: Heinemann.

Simon, H. 1974. "How Big Is a Chunk?" *Science* 183: 482–88.

Sipe, R. B. 2003. *They Still Can't Spell?* Portsmouth, NH: Heinemann.

Smith, D. 2004. *The Gingerbread Boy Play.* Access at *www.reudingludy.com/Readers_Theater/Scripts/The_Gingerbread_Boy_Play.doc*.

Smith, F. 1988. *Joining the Literacy Club: Further Essays into Education*. Portsmouth, NH: Heinemann.

———. 1994. *Understanding Reading: A Psycholinguistic Analysis of Reading and Learning to Read*, 5th ed. Hillsdale, NJ: Erlbaum.

Stauffer, R. 1980. *The Language Experience Approach to the Teaching of Reading*, 2d ed. New York: Harper & Row.

Strickland, D. S., and L. Morrow. 1990. "Family Literacy: Sharing Good Books." *The Reading Teacher* 43: 518–19.

Strickland, K. 1995. *Literacy, Not Labels*. Portsmouth, NH: Heinemann.

Strickland, K., and J. Strickland. 2000. *Making Assessment Elementary*. Portsmouth, NH: Heinemann.

Vacca, R. T., J. A. Vacca, and M. K. Gove. 1995. *Reading and Learning to Read*, 3d ed. New York: HarperCollins.

Vygotsky, L. 1978. *Mind in Society: The Development of Higher Psychological Processes*. Cambridge, MA: Harvard University Press.

Weaver, C. 2002. *Reading Process and Practice*, 3d ed. Portsmouth, NH: Heinemann.

Wilde, S. 2000. *Miscue Analysis Made Easy: Building on Student Strengths*. Portsmouth, NH: Heinemann.

Wylie, R. E., and D. D. Durrell. 1970. "Teaching Vowels Through Phonograms." *Elementary English* 47: 787–91.

Index